OXFORD PICTURE DICTIONARY

for the Canadian Content Areas

Dorothy Kauffman
Gary Apple

OXFORD
UNIVERSITY PRESS

OXFORD
UNIVERSITY PRESS

8 Sampson Mews, Suite 204, Don Mills, Ontario M3C 0H5
www.oupcanada.com

Oxford University Press is a department of the University of Oxford.
It furthers the University's objective of excellence in research, scholarship,
and education by publishing worldwide in

Oxford   New York

Auckland Cape Town Dar es Salaam Hong Kong Karachi
Kuala Lumpur Madrid Melbourne Mexico City Nairobi
New Delhi Shanghai Taipei Toronto

With offices in

Argentina Austria Brazil Chile Czech Republic France Greece
Guatemala Hungary Italy Japan Poland Portugal Singapore
South Korea Switzerland Thailand Turkey Ukraine Vietnam

Oxford is a trade mark of Oxford University Press
in the UK and in certain other countries

Published in Canada
by Oxford University Press

Oxford Picture Dictionary for the Content Areas was originally published
in 2010. This edition is published by arrangement with Oxford University
Press, Inc., 198 Madison Avenue, New York, N.Y. 10016-4314, USA.

Library and Archives Canada Cataloguing in Publication

Kauffman, Dorothy, 1942-
Oxford picture dictionary for the Canadian content areas /
Dorothy Kauffman, Gary Apple.
Includes bibliographical references and index.

ISBN 978-0-19-544005-8

1. English language—Textbooks for second language learners.
2. Picture dictionaries, English—Juvenile literature. I. Apple, Gary II. Title.

PE1128.K375 2010   j423'.17   C2010-902148-7

This book is printed on permanent (acid-free) paper. ∞

Printed and bound in Canada.

6 7 – 16 15

ACKNOWLEDGEMENTS

Illustrations by: Wendy Wassink Ackison: 18-19, 22, (ambulance, paramedic), 97 (girl, students); Garin Baker: 8-9, 179, 181; Thomas Bayley: 56-57 (#11-15, city scene); Steven Talmond Brown: 96-97 (skeleton, body parts), 100 (muscle, jaw, lungs); Rob Burman: 38-39 (corn, grain elevator, wheat); Dan Burr: 10-11; Uldis Clavins: 40-41 (#1-4, 7), 50 (dam), 68-69 (#1, 2); Mona Diane Conner: 106-107, 126-127, 132 (plants, chicken); Leela Corman: Talk About It - 22, 50, 62, 82, 92, 100, 132, 144, 158, 176; Robert Crawford: 4-5, 16-17, 22 (office, gym, principal, coach); 48-49 (#11, 14, 15), Dom D'Andrea: 28 (#6-10) 34-35 (#1-4, 6), 36-37 (#1, 2, 7); Grace DeVito: 110-113, 118-119, 132 (mushroom, bee); John Edwards: 56-57 #11-18; Jim Effler: 114 (#4-8), 115 (top two right), 122-123, 126 (pig), 132 (frog), 152-153, 160-161; Russell Farrell: 128-129 (except #6, 7), 132 (elephant); Jeff Foster: 160-163; Michael Garland: 6-7; John Paul Genzo: 114 (#1-3, 9-14), 115 (top left, bottom), 116-117, 120-121, 130-131, 132 (worm, protozoan, clam, goldfish); Geosystems Global Corp.: 182-183; David Henderson: 14-15; 56-57 (#1-9); Ink Link: 54-55 (#1-6), 58-59, 62 (Ancient China); Aleta Jenks: 168-169; John Kaufmann: 143 (bottom), 144 (electricity), 146-149, 150-151 (#17- 20), 156-157, 156 (top six spots), 157; Manuel Larino: 20-21, 22 (police officer, mail carrier), 142-143 (#1-13), 144 (sound, light, heat); Jerry LoFaro: 150-151 (#1-16), Alan Male: 124-125; William Maughan: 78-79 (#3, 7-11); Shawn McKelvey: 136-137, 170-171, 174-175; Karen Minot: 44-47; Tom Newsom: 12-13, 22 (police station, post office); Laurie O'Keefe: 104-105, 118-119 (tick), 132 (monerans); Craig Orback: 166-167; Terry Paczko: 140-141, 154-155, 156 (pollution, smog); Janet Pietrobono: 180 (thick/thin, full/empty, dirty/clean); Stephanie Pershing: 102-103, 108-109; Bill Schmidt: 94-95, 98-99 (# 2, 3, 5, 6, 8, 9, 11-13, 15, 16),

100 (leg, hand, arm, mouth, eye, finger); Rob Schuster: 23, 51 (laptop), 101 (fruits, vegetables), 132 (tree), 133, 145, 176 (left) -175; Tim Spransy: 178 (top); Taylor Stamper: 179 (top); Ron Tanovitz: 98 (#4, 7, 10, 14), 100 (taste, sight, touch); Ralph Voltz: 2-3, 134-135, 144 (liquid, solid, gas, mixture, compound, element), 172-173. Haywiremedia/Shutterstock: 22, 50, 62, 82, 92, 100, 132, 144, 158, 176 (web browser).

Maps: ArtPlus Limited

All other illustrations: Lynn Shwadchuck

Thank you to the following for granting permission to use the logos on pages 90 and 91:

The Commonwealth; Organization of the American States; Asia-Pacific Economic Cooperation (The APEC Logo is reproduced with the permission of the APEC Secretariat, Singapore. For more information, please visit www.apec.org.); United Nations; International Olympic Committee; UNICEF; Canadian Red Cross; Habitat for Humanity International (Habitat for Humanity is an independent nonprofit organization.)

Thank you also to the Bloc Québécois, the Conservative Party of Canada, the New Democratic Party of Canada, and the Liberal Party of Canada for permission to their logos on pages 84 and 85.

Dorothy Kauffman, Ph.D., is a consultant with the Center for Applied Linguistics (CAL) in Washington, D.C. Through CAL, she advocates for instruction that integrates the teaching of language and content, and she conducts professional development workshops with K–8 ESL and mainstream teachers. A former elementary school teacher, reading teacher, and reading consultant, she has taught speech, reading, and English composition at the college level. At the university level, she has taught reading and language arts methods courses and children's literature, and also has supervised student teachers in elementary and middle schools. At the graduate level, she has developed and taught courses in reading and ESL methods.

Program Consultant: Kate Kinsella, Ed.D.
Content Area Consultants: Jeff Passe, Ph.D., Julie A. Luft, Ph.D.,
Vena M. Long, Ed.D.
Language Proficiency Standards Expert: Margo Gottlieb, Ph.D.
Advisory Committee: Mary Lou McCloskey, Ph.D., JoAnn (Jodi) Crandall, Ph.D., Tonya Ward Singer, Cecilia Silva, Ph.D., Maria N. Trejo, Ed.D.

**Oxford University Press Canada would like to extend a special thank-you to
our Canadian reviewers:**
Tara Giguere, Sherida Hassanali, Sharon MacNeice, Tony Moscone, and
Catherine Pawis

**We would also like to thank the following people for their suggestions
along the way:**

Lidija Biro	Judith Ngan
Alison Boyer	Maggie Perquin
Nora Buta	Laurie Peters
Pippa Creery	Lisa Rochman
Cecelia Gamboa	Karen Roth
Darren Horn	Marlene Saavedra
Claire Hughes	Dorothy Schmauder
Catherine Humphries	Cecilia Song
Matthew Jackson	Brandie Spanos
Anne-Marie Kaskens	Deb Weber
Diane Kim	Sonny Wilson
Ruthanne Leach	Alice Wong
Susan Likar	Beth Woods
Aurelia Loschiavo	Sheetal Woods
Nancy Musica	

A big thank-you to Breanne MacDonald for her help with research and layout.
—Cindy

For four people who made a difference ... Margaret Peters, for a sense of the classical; Nancy Larrick, for a sense of the enchanting; Jessie Roderick, for a sense of the ethical; and Gail Alwine, for a sense of the rational.
—dotti

OXFORD PICTURE DICTIONARY
for the Canadian Content Areas

Topic pages combine curriculum-based content vocabulary and the academic language that learners need to be successful.

Curriculum-Based

Curriculum-based topics support the content learners will encounter in content-area classes.

Academic Language

Exercises model and practise academic language and grammar using the topic's content vocabulary.

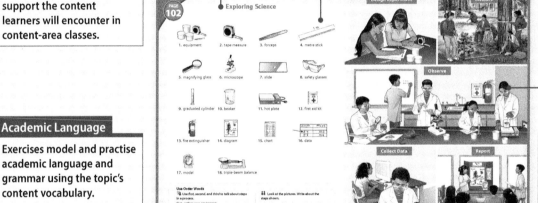

Clear images provide visual meaning to support each content-area term.

Rich, vibrant images showcase topic vocabulary in real-world contexts, allowing students to make meaningful connections.

Unit Expansion pages develop academic reading, writing, speaking, and listening skills using content-area vocabulary.

Reading and Writing

Graphic organizers aid pre-writing and content-area readings model effective writing using unit vocabulary.

Speaking and Listening

Speaking and listening exercises promote oral language development.

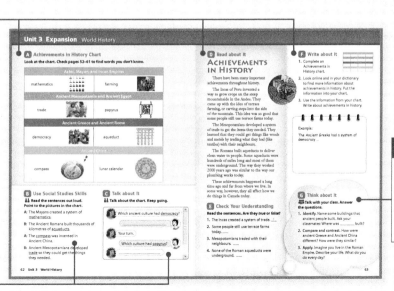

Critical Thinking

Questions prompt learners to use higher-level cognitive skills while practising oral language and vocabulary.

Teaching with the *Oxford Picture Dictionary for the Canadian Content Areas*

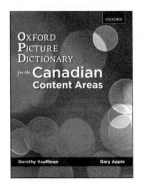

There are many different ways that you can use the *Oxford Picture Dictionary for the Canadian Content Areas* to support language and concept development. Within each topic, you can comprehensively teach all terms or selectively address those that directly correlate to your curriculum. In either scenario, use this explicit and interactive routine to teach the topic words. A consistent routine engages students in a familiar and accountable process, allowing them to devote their full attention to new concepts rather than new directions.

Introduce the Topic

- Give a brief introduction. For example:

  Today we are going to learn about <u>weather words</u>. Our new topic is <u>weather</u>.

Build Background

- Have students scan the term list to identify terms they may already know. *You may already know some of these words. Look at the pictures. Find one or two words you already know.*

- Write this sentence starter on the board:
  I know this word in English. This is _____.
  Model the response: *I know this word in English. This is <u>rain</u>.*

- Introduce the starter and model a correct response. *We will use this starter to share with partners. Listen as I read it aloud. Now, let's read it together. Add the word you know to the end of the sentence. For example, I added rain. I will tell my partner "I know this word in English. This is <u>rain</u>."*

- Begin structured partner interaction. *Now point to one of the words you already know and tell your partner you know this word. Use the starter. Let's begin.* If your students are new to partnering, model how to share ideas with a partner using a starter.

- Monitor partner interactions. As students share, listen for topic terms they correctly recognize. Also take note of common confusions. It is possible that students will point out objects in a picture that are not the actual focus term. For example, for the picture of *sleet*, students might say they know the word *leaf* or *tree*. Rather than trying to redirect students' attention to the appropriate focus in a picture, write down these misunderstandings so that you can address them to the whole class.

- Introduce each term. *Now let's look at each word and find the ones we already know. Number _____ is _____. Point to _____. Show me a thumbs up if you know the word, or a thumbs down if you don't.* (Model thumb up/down.)

- Note which terms the students recognize. Write those terms on the board. Begin with these more familiar terms when you teach the word meanings.

Prepare to Teach

- First, determine the vocabulary you will teach to meet your instructional objectives. For example, if you are preparing students for a science lesson on weather, choose only the topic terms that directly support that lesson.

- Next, consider the level of complexity of the terms you intend to teach. Each topic includes both concrete terms that can be taught quickly with a picture (e.g., *cloud*, *lightning*) as well as more abstract, conceptual terms that require in-depth instruction (e.g., *evaporation*, *condensation*).

- Finally, group terms for instruction. Each topic list includes a larger quantity than students can digest in one class session. It is important to teach the terms in manageable clusters. For the concrete and easily depicted terms, you may be able to cover 6–8 in a lesson. However, you may have to devote an entire lesson to more challenging concept terms. Consider teaching together:

  - terms students already identified as familiar
  - terms that have a clear conceptual link
  - terms that are the same part of speech
  - terms that can be applied in the partner task in the exercise banner

Teach

- Introduce the term. For example: *Our first word is* tornado. *Point to* number 4, tornado. *Let's say it together:* tornado. *Now let's tap out the syllables as we say it again:* tor•na•do. *One more time, quickly:* tornado.

- Name the part of speech and rephrase it in student-friendly language: _____ *is a* _____ *(noun: a person, place, thing, or idea; verb: an action word; adjective: a describing word).*

- Teach with the picture. First, explain how the picture shows the term. If there is more than one object in the picture, be sure to focus students' attention on the representation of the target term. For example: *Point to picture number 4, a tornado. There is a building in this picture, but I want you to focus on the grey area that looks like a cloud. This is a tornado. Now point to the tornado and say with me, "This is a tornado."*

- Explain the term. For more complex terms, complement the picture with explicit explanation, gestures, and modelling. When possible, support your explanation by referring to images in the contextualized scene opposite the term list. To ensure listening comprehension, use everyday words to clarify meaning rather than precise technical language.

- Check comprehension. After teaching a group of terms in one lesson, do a quick review. Say the terms one at a time in a new order and have students point to the appropriate picture on either page. (e.g., *Find* fog. *Point to a picture of* fog). Follow with a quick partner interaction. Partner A points to the scene on the right and names a term. Partner B determines whether this is correct.

  A: This is _____.

  B: Yes, that's right. That is _____.

  or

  No, that's not right. (Pointing to the correct picture) This is _____.

Teach the Language Objective with the Exercise Banner

- Read the title of the exercise banner and state the purpose of the task. Then have students point to the directions and read them orally with you.

- Teach key grammatical concepts students will need to complete the task.

- Read each model sentence twice. First read it aloud, then have students read it chorally with you. To ensure comprehension, have students point to the appropriate picture(s).

- Explain the partner task. Have students point to the directions and read them orally with you.

- Read aloud the model answer and the first sentence frame. Explain what is necessary to complete the task.

- Model the partner process. Pair students. Indicate which partner will share first.

- Monitor student responses and re-teach as needed. If students are successful with the initial task, have them continue completing the sentences with their partners. If students are struggling, model and guide practice.

- After partners interact, call on individuals to share with the whole group.

- To provide additional practice, have students write their responses in a notebook.

Beginning English learners need daily opportunities to flex their English language muscles in meaningful academic contexts. We trust these engaging, research-based instructional routines will bolster students' content knowledge and accelerate their language development.

Kate Kinsella, Ed.D.

Kate Kinsella, Ed.D.

Tonya Ward Singer

Tonya Ward Singer

Research Bibliography

Research and Reports

August, D., & Shanahan, T. (Eds.). (2006). *Developing literacy in second-language learners: Report of the National Literacy Panel on Language-minority Children and Youth*. Mahwah, NJ: Lawrence Erlbaum Associates.

August, D., & Shanahan, T. (Eds.). (2008). *Developing reading and writing in second-language learners: Lessons from the report of the National Literacy Panel on Language-minority Children and Youth*. New York: Routledge.

Biancarosa, G., & Snow, C. E. (2006). *Reading next: A vision for action and research in middle and high school literacy: A report to Carnegie Corporation of New York*. (2nd ed.). Washington, DC: Alliance for Excellent Education.

Genesee, F., Lindholm-Leary, K., Saunders, W., & Christian, D. (2006). *Educating English language learners: A synthesis of research evidence*. New York: Cambridge University Press.

Grabe, W., & Stoller, F. L. (2002). *Teaching and researching reading*. Harlow, England: Pearson Education.

Hirsch, Jr., E. D. (2006). *The knowledge deficit: Closing the shocking education gap for American children*. Boston: Houghton Mifflin.

Kamil, M. L. (2003). *Adolescents and literacy: Reading for the 21st century*. Washington, DC: Alliance for Excellent Education.

Morrow, L. M., Gambrell, L. B., & Pressley, M. (Eds.). (2003). *Best practices in literacy instruction*. (2nd ed.). New York: Guilford Press.

Padrón, Y., Waxman, H., & Rivera, H. (2002). *Educating Hispanic students: Obstacles and avenues to improved academic achievement. Educational Practice Report 8*. Santa Cruz, CA: Center for Research on Education, Diversity & Excellence.

Short, D. J., & Fitzsimmons, S. (2007). *Double the work: Challenges and solutions to acquiring language and academic literacy for adolescent English language learners – A report to Carnegie Corporation of New York*. Washington, DC: Alliance for Excellent Education.

Thomas, W. P., & Collier, V. P. (2002). *A national study of school effectiveness for language minority students' long-term academic achievement*. Santa Cruz, CA: Center for Research on Education, Diversity & Excellence.

Unsworth, L. (2001). *Teaching multiliteracies across the curriculum: Changing contexts of text and image in classroom practice*. Buckingham, UK: Open University Press.

Teaching Vocabulary, Reading, Academic Content, and Study Skills

Calderón, M. (2007). *Teaching reading to English language learners, Grades 6–12: A framework for improving achievement in the content areas*. Thousand Oaks, CA: Corwin Press.

Center for the Improvement of Early Reading Achievement (CIERA). (2001). *Teaching every child to read: Frequently asked questions*. Available from http://www.ciera.org/library/instresrc/tecr/index.html

Chamot, A.U. (2009). *The CALLA handbook: Implementing the cognitive academic language learning approach*. (2nd ed.). White Plains, NY: Pearson Longman.

Crandall, J., Jaramillo, A., Olsen, L., Peyton, J. K., & Young, S. (2001). Diverse teaching strategies for immigrant and refugee children. In R.W. Cole (Ed.), *Educating everybody's children: More teaching strategies for diverse learners* (pp. 219–278). Alexandria, VA: Association for Supervision and Curriculum Development.

Dutro, S. (2005). *What's language got to do with it? Considerations in courses of study for secondary English learners*. Available from http://www.elachieve.org

Echevarria, J., Vogt, M., & Short, D. J. (2008). *Making content comprehensible for English learners: The SIOP model* (3rd ed.). Boston: Allyn & Bacon.

Fathman, A. K., & Crowther, D. T. (Eds.). (2006). *Science for English language learners: K–12 classroom strategies*. Arlington, VA: National Science Teachers Association.

Fillmore, L. W., & Snow, C. E. (2002). What teachers need to know about language. In C. T. Adger, C. E. Snow, and D. Christian (Eds.), *What teachers need to know about language* (pp. 7–53). McHenry, IL: Delta Systems.

Fitzgerald, J., & Graves, M. F. (2004). *Scaffolding reading experiences for English-language learners*. Norwood, MA: Christopher-Gordon.

Fountas, I. C., & Pinnell, G. S. (2001). *Guiding readers and writers, grades 3–6: Teaching comprehension, genre, and content literacy*. Portsmouth, NH: Heinemann.

Gibbons, P. (2003). Mediating language learning: Teacher interactions with ESL students in a content-based classroom. *TESOL Quarterly, 37*, 247–273.

Grognet, A., Jameson, J., Franco, L., & Derrick-Mescua, M. (2000). *Enhancing English language learning in elementary classrooms*. McHenry, IL: Delta Systems.

Harvey, S., & Goudvis, A. (2000). *Strategies That Work*. Portland, ME: Stenhouse Publishers.

Herrell, A. L., & Jordan, M. (2007). *Fifty strategies for teaching English language learners* (3rd ed.). Upper Saddle River, NJ: Pearson Education.

Irujo, S. (Ed.). (2000). *Integrating the ESL standards into classroom practice: Grades 6–8*. Alexandria, VA: Teachers of English to Speakers of Other Languages.

Jameson, J. (1998). *Enriching content classes for secondary ESOL students*. McHenry, IL: Delta Systems.

Kamil, M. L., & Hiebert, E. H. (2005). Teaching and learning vocabulary: Perspectives and persistent issues. In E. H. Heibert & Kamil, M. L. (Eds.), *Teaching and learning vocabulary: Bringing research to practice*. Mahwah, NJ: Erlbaum.

Kauffman, D. (2007). *What's different about teaching reading to students learning English?* Washington, DC: Center for Applied Linguistics.

Keene, E. O., & Zimmerman, S. (2007). *Mosaic of thought: The power of comprehension strategy instruction* (2nd ed.). Portsmouth, NH: Heinemann.

Kinsella, K. (2007). *Academic language development strategies that boost literacy and learning across all subject areas*. Paper presented at Missouri Migrant Education and English Language Learning (MELL) Conference, St. Louis, MO.

Lacina, J., New Levine, L., & Sowa, P. (Ed.). (2007). *Helping English language learners succeed in pre-K–elementary schools*. Alexandria, VA: Teachers of English to Speakers of Other Languages.

Lehr, F., & Osborn, J. (2005). *A focus on comprehension*. Honolulu, HI: Pacific Resources for Education and Learning.

Melzer, J., & Hamann, E. T. (2004). *Meeting the literacy development needs of adolescent English language learners through content area learning. Part one: Focus on motivation and engagement*. Providence, RI: Brown University.

Melzer, J., & Hamann, E. T. (2005). *Meeting the literacy development needs of adolescent English language learners through content area learning. Part two: Focus on classroom teaching and learning strategies*. Providence, RI: Brown University.

New Levine, L., & McCloskey, M. L. (2009). *Teaching learners of English in mainstream classrooms (K–8): One class, many paths*. Boston: Allyn & Bacon.

Peregoy, S. F., & Boyle, O. F. (2008). *Reading, writing, and learning in ESL: A resource book for teaching K–12 English learners* (5th ed.). Boston: Allyn & Bacon.

Richard-Amato, P. A., & Snow, M. A. (Eds.). (2005). *Academic success for English language learners: Strategies for K–12 mainstream teachers*. White Plains, NY: Pearson Education.

Tankersley, K. (2005). *Literacy strategies for grades 4–12: Reinforcing the threads of reading*. Alexandria, VA: Association for Supervision and Curriculum Development.

Tovani, C. (2000). *I read it, but I don't get it: Comprehension strategies for adolescent readers*. Portland, ME: Stenhouse Publishers.

Standards References

Center for Research on Education, Diversity & Excellence. (2001). *The CREDE five standards for effective pedagogy and learning*. Available from http://crede.berkeley.edu/research/crede/standards.html

Core Knowledge Foundation. (1999). *Core knowledge sequence: Content guidelines for grades K–8*. Charlottesville, VA: Author.

Lowery, L. F. (Ed.). (2000). *NSTA pathways to the science standards: Guidelines for moving the vision into practice, elementary school edition*. (2nd ed.). Arlington, VA: National Science Teachers Association.

National Center for History in the Schools. (n.d.). *National standards for world history: Exploring paths to the present*. Grades 5–12 expanded edition. Los Angeles: University of California.

National Council for the Social Studies. (1994). *Expectations of excellence: Curriculum standards for social studies*. Silver Spring, MD: Author.

National Council of Teachers of Mathematics. (2000). *Principles and standards for school mathematics*. Reston, VA: Author.

Teachers of English to Speakers of Other Languages. (2006). *PreK-12 English language proficiency standards*. Alexandria, VA: Author.

Texley, J., & Wild, A. (Eds.). (2004). *NSTA pathways to the science standards: Guidelines for moving the vision into practice, second high school edition*. Arlington, VA: National Science Teachers Association.

World-Class Instructional Design and Assessment (WIDA) Consortium. (2007). *English language proficiency standards*. Available from WIDA Consortium Web site, http://wida.wceruw.org/standards/elp.aspx

Table of Contents

Unit 8	The Physical World

Unit 9	Earth and Space Science

Unit 10	Math and Technology

Appendix

The Classroom

 1. teacher

 2. student

 3. desk

 4. table

 5. chair

 6 book

 7. notebook

 8. paper

 9. pencil

 10. pen

 11. crayon

 12. pencil sharpener

 13. ruler

 14. glue

 15. computer

 16. map

 17. whiteboard

 18. bulletin board

 19. blackboard

 20. wastebasket

Count More Than One

Add *s* to many nouns to show there are more than one.

student + s = students

1 student ⟶ 10 students

pencil + s = pencils

1 pencil ⟶ 8 pencils

Look at the picture. Talk about what you see.
Examples:
I see two maps.
I see four chairs.

The School

1. principal

2. secretary

3. librarian

4. coach

5. custodian/ caretaker

6. office

7. library

8. cafeteria/ lunchroom

9. gym

10. auditorium

11. media centre

12. playground

13. locker

14. hall

15. stairs

16. drinking fountain

17. boys' room

18. girls' room

Where Is It?

Ask *Where is the …?* to find a place.

Where is the library?

The library is on the third floor.

Where is the office?

The office is on the first floor.

3rd floor
2nd floor
1st floor

Look at the picture. Ask and answer questions about places in the school.

Examples :

Where is the auditorium?

Where is the cafeteria?

The House

1. kitchen

2. living room

3. bathroom

4. bedroom

5. attic

6. basement

7. window

8. door

9. wall

10. floor

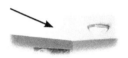

11. ceiling

12. closet

13. sink

14. toilet

15. bathtub

16. shower

17. cupboard

18. porch

19. roof

20. chimney

Talk about Location

Use *in the* … to answer questions about locations.

Where is the sink?

The sink is <u>in the</u> bathroom.

Where is the closet?

The closet is <u>in the</u> bedroom.

Look at the picture. Ask and answer questions about what you see.

Examples:

Where is the bed?

Where is the shower?

The Family

1. grandparents

2. grandmother

3. grandfather

4. parents

5. mother

6. father

7. baby

8. sister

9. brother

10. aunt

11. uncle

12. cousins

Other Family Members

This family tree shows some family members, but not all.
You may have a half-brother who shares one of your
parents but not both. You could have a stepsister if one
of your parents remarried someone who had a daughter.
Some people have only one parent and some people do
not have all the relatives in the picture. You may have two
mothers or two fathers instead of a mother and a father.

👥 **Draw a picture of your family.**
Draw your family and show it to a classmate.
Explain who each member is.

Feelings

1. sick

2. tired

3. thirsty

4. hot

5. cold

6. hungry

7. silly

8. shy

9. scared

10. surprised

11. proud

12. sad

13. happy

14. lonely

15. excited

16. angry

Write about Feelings

Use adjectives to describe feelings.

The boy feels <u>shy</u>.

The clown feels <u>sad</u>.

The girl feels <u>scared</u>.

The boy feels <u>proud</u>.

Look at the pictures. Think about what gives people these feelings. Ask a classmate.

Examples:

Why do people feel hungry?

Why do people feel surprised?

Unit 1   General Knowledge

The City (Urban Area)

1. restaurant

2. hotel

3. post office

4. department store

5. office building

6. apartment building

7. bank

8. movie theatre

9. police station

10. church

11. mosque

12. temple

13. parking garage

14. subway

15. bus

16. taxi

17. helicopter

18. garbage truck

19. ATM (automated teller machine)

20. traffic light

Where Is It?

Use *close to* and *far from* to describe where something is.

A ↔ B   A is close to B
C ↔ D   C is far from D

The garbage truck is <u>close to</u> the bank.

The taxi is <u>far from</u> the church.

The subway is <u>close to</u> the movie theatre.

The temple is <u>far from</u> the restaurant.

Look at the picture. Talk about the city.
Examples:

The subway is close to the police station.

The department store is far from the restaurant.

The Suburbs

1. street

2. sidewalk

3. crosswalk

4. corner

5. block

6. yard

7. driveway

8. garage

9. garden

10. swimming pool

11. park

12. gas station

13. stop sign

14. mailbox

15. fire hydrant

16. van

 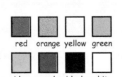 

17. car

18. motorcycle

19. bicycle

20. basketball

Describe with Colour

Use colour words to describe nouns.

There is a <u>red</u> mailbox.
There are <u>green</u> yards.
The car is <u>blue</u>.
The houses are <u>white</u>.

red orange yellow green
blue purple black white

Look around the neighbourhood you are in. Write about colours you see.
Examples:
There is a green car.
The garage is orange.

The Country (Rural Area)

1. farm

2. barn

3. silo

4. chicken coop

5. fence

6. path

7. orchard

8. pasture

9. pond

10. woods

11. hills

12. field

13. road

14. stream

15. bridge

16. airplane

17. train

18. truck

19. tractor

20. wagon

Inside or Outside?

📝 Use *inside* or *outside* to describe where something is.

The horse is <u>inside</u> the barn.

The children are <u>inside</u> the wagon.

The woman is <u>outside</u> the house.

The cows are <u>outside</u> the barn.

inside   outside

👥 Look at the picture. Talk about the country.

Examples:

The tractor is outside the barn.

The bridge is outside the farm.

The Hospital

 1. patient

 2. doctor

 3. nurse

 4. paramedic

 5. examination table

 6. bed

 7. pillow

 8. blanket

 9. X-ray

 10. stethoscope

 11. thermometer

 12. medicine

 13. bandage

 14. cast

 15. crutches

 16. wheelchair

 17. stretcher

 18. ambulance

Write about the Present

Use *is* and an action verb + *ing* to describe what people are doing now.

The doctor <u>is listening</u> to her heart.
The boy <u>is walking</u> with crutches.
The patient <u>is wearing</u> a bandage.
The woman <u>is holding</u> the baby.

Look at the picture. Write about people at the hospital.

Examples:
The nurse is helping the boy.
The paramedic is pulling the stretcher.

Unit 1   General Knowledge

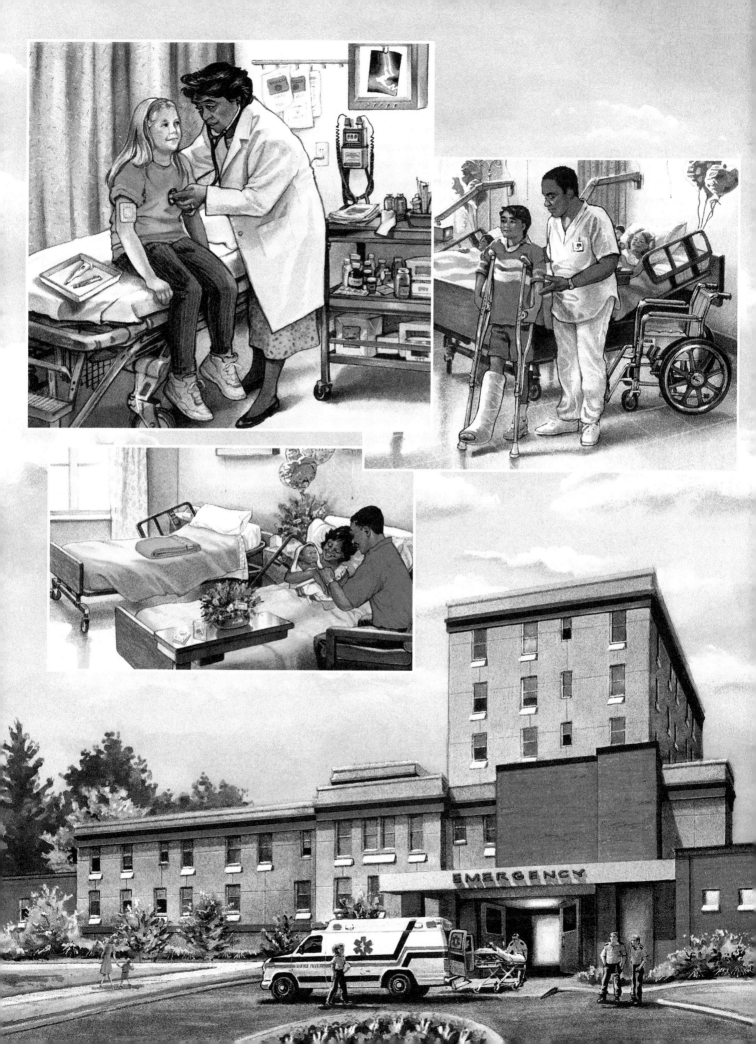

EMERGENCY

People at Work

1. construction worker

2. electrician

3. carpenter

4. mail carrier

5. firefighter

6. police officer

7. mechanic

8. messenger

9. musician

10. painter

11. computer programmer

12. writer

13. dentist

14. dental assistant

15. hairdresser

16. plumber

17. pharmacist

18. salesperson

Describe Jobs

Use a present tense verb to talk about what people do at their jobs.

A musician <u>plays</u> music.

A mechanic <u>fixes</u> cars.

A dental assistant <u>cleans</u> teeth.

A salesperson <u>sells</u> things.

Look at the picture. Talk about jobs.

Examples:

A writer writes books.

A plumber fixes plumbing.

A Jobs and Workplaces Chart

Look at the chart. Check pages 2–21 to find words you don't know.

A Place to Work	Where It Is	A Job People Do There
office	the school	principal
gym		coach
police station	the city	police officer
post office		mail carrier
ambulance	the hospital	paramedic

B Use Social Studies Skills

👥 **Read the sentences out loud. Point to the pictures in the chart.**

A: The <u>principal</u> works in the <u>office</u>.

B: The <u>mail carrier</u> works in the <u>post office</u>.

A: The <u>paramedic</u> works in the <u>ambulance</u>.

B: The <u>coach</u> works in the <u>gym</u>.

A: The <u>police officer</u> works in the <u>police station</u>.

C Talk about It

👥 **Ask and answer questions about the chart. Keep going.**

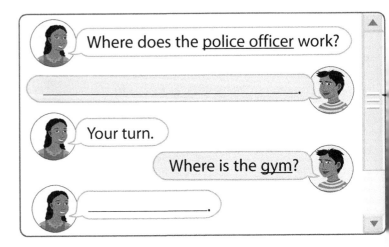

Where does the <u>police officer</u> work?

Your turn.

Where is the <u>gym</u>?

D Read about It

Jobs and Workplaces

People have many kinds of jobs. They work in different places. Some people work in schools. Teachers, principals, and librarians work in schools. Doctors work in hospitals. Nurses work in hospitals, too.

Sometimes people work in many places. Mail carriers work in post offices. They also carry mail to houses, department stores, and banks. Police officers work in police stations. They also work on city streets. People do important jobs in all these places.

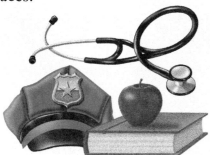

E Check Your Understanding

Read the sentences. Are they *true* or *false*?

1. There are many kinds of jobs. __T__

2. Teachers work in schools. ____

3. Principals work in banks. ____

4. Librarians work in hospitals. ____

5. Doctors work in hospitals. ____

6. Nurses work in department stores. ____

7. Mail carriers work in post offices. ____

8. Mail carriers do not go to houses. ____

9. Police officers work in banks. ____

10. Police officers do not work on city streets. ____

F Write about It

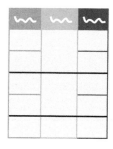

1. Complete a Jobs and Workplaces chart. Choose any jobs you know about.

2. Find more people and jobs in your dictionary. Write the words or draw pictures in your chart.

3. Write about your Jobs and Workplaces chart.

Example:

Lawyers work in courthouses. They work in offices, too. Secretaries also work in offices ...

G Think about It

Talk with your class. Answer the questions.

1. **Make associations.** Classmate A: Name a place where people work. Classmate B: Say one job people do there. Take turns.

2. **Apply.** What job do you want to do? Why?

3. **Compare and contrast.** How is a teacher's job similar to a doctor's job? How is it different?

Canadian Provinces, Territories, and Bodies of Water

AB Alberta

BC British Columbia

MB Manitoba

NB New Brunswick

NL Newfoundland and Labrador

NT Northwest Territories

NS Nova Scotia

NU Nunavut

ON Ontario

PE Prince Edward Island

QC Quebec

SK Saskatchewan

YT Yukon

Arctic Ocean

Atlantic Ocean

Pacific Ocean

Hudson Bay

Great Lakes

Lake Erie

Lake Huron

Lake Michigan

Lake Ontario

Lake Superior

Talk about Directions

Use *north*, *south*, *east*, and *west* to describe location.

Lake Superior is <u>north</u> of Lake Michigan.
Manitoba is <u>south</u> of Nunavut.
New Brunswick is <u>east</u> of Quebec.
British Columbia is <u>west</u> of Alberta.

Look at the map. Talk about the provinces, territories, and bodies of water.

A: Yukon is west of _____.
B: Quebec is _____ of Ontario.
A: Saskatchewan is _____ of _____.
B: _____ is _____ of _____.

Canadian Provinces and Territories

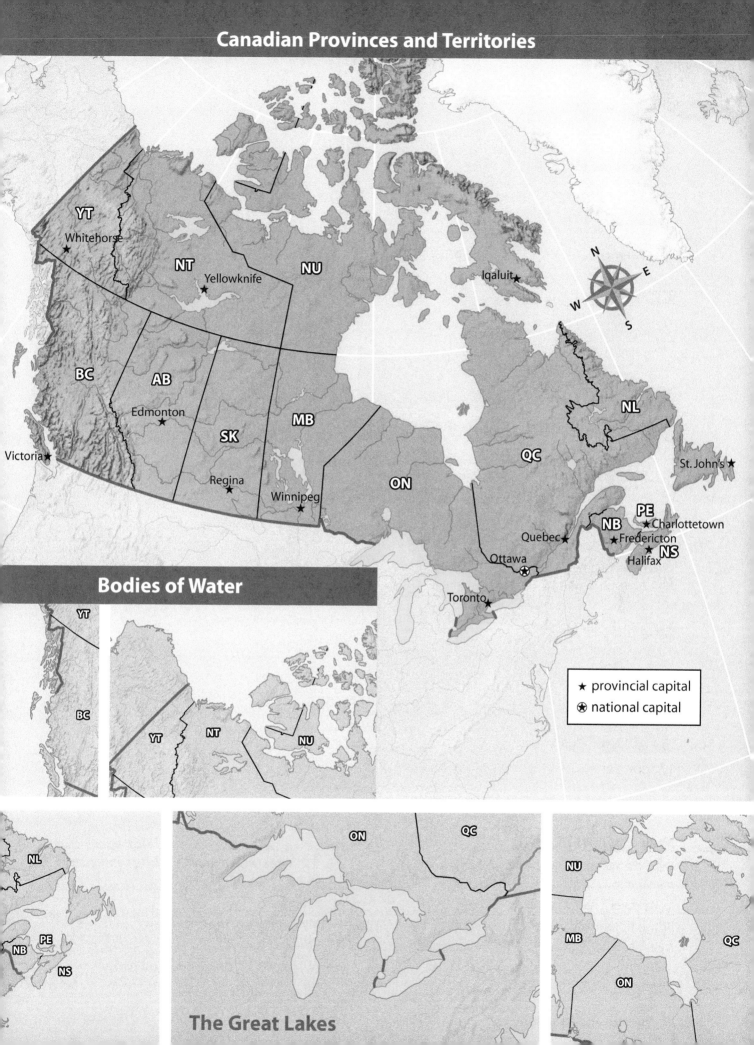

YT
Whitehorse ★

NT
Yellowknife ★

NU

Iqaluit ★

BC

AB
Edmonton ★

SK
Regina ★

MB
Winnipeg ★

NL

QC

ON

Victoria ★

N
W — E
S

St. John's ★

PE
★ Charlottetown
NB
Fredericton ★
NS
Halifax

Quebec ★

Ottawa ⊛

Toronto ★

★ provincial capital
⊛ national capital

Bodies of Water

YT

BC

YT   NT   NU

The Great Lakes

NL

NB   PE
NS

ON   QC

NU

MB   QC

ON

Pacific Coast

1. Western Cordillera

2. Interior Plateau

3. Rocky Mountains

4. Vancouver Island

5. Haida Gwaii

6. Okanagan Valley

7. Fraser River

8. orchard

9. totem pole

10. grizzly bear

11. salmon

12. seal

13. cougar

Show Ownership

📇 Add 's to a person, place, or thing to show ownership.

My brother's name is Dan.

British Columbia's capital city is Victoria.

A grizzly bear's diet includes salmon.

👥 Work with a partner. Write sentences to show ownership.

Examples:

My mother's name is Linda.

Canada's capital is Ottawa.

A salmon's scales are grey and pink.

The Prairies

1. Interior Plains

2. foothills

3. Drumheller

4. Dinosaur Provincial Park

5. hoodoo

6. ranch

7. cattle

8. rodeo

9. cowboy

10. cowgirl

11. oil sands

12. machinery

13. RCMP Heritage Centre

14. Royal Canadian Mounted Police

15. soapstone carvings

16. bison

17. black bear

18. beluga whale

Make a Chart

Many compound words are one word.

| cow | + | boy | = | cowboy |
| foot | + | hills | = | foothills |

Some compound words are two words.

| oil | + | sands | = | oil sands |

Write the compound words and the words that are not compound words.

Compound Words	Not Compound Words
cowgirl	bison
_____	_____

Central Canada

1. Canadian Shield

2. Great Lakes–St. Lawrence Lowlands

3. St. Lawrence River

4. Appalachians

5. Niagara Falls

6. CN Tower

7. Rogers Centre

8. skyscraper

9. tourist

10. highway

11. Quebec Winter Carnival/Carnaval de Québec

12. Bonhomme Carnaval

13. sugar shack

14. maple syrup

15. sap

16. tap

17. fox

18. moose

19. wolf

20. beaver

Think about the Topic

There are many places in Canada where tourists like to visit. In Toronto, the CN Tower is one of the most popular tourist attractions. A busy time to be in Quebec City is during the Carnaval de Québec, which is held in the winter. People love to see the snow sculptures, visit the ice palace, and skate with the carnival's mascot, Bonhomme Carnaval.

Talk about these questions. Make a list of your answers.

What are some places in your city that tourists like to visit? What about in your province? Are there any tourist attractions in other provinces that you have visited? Did you enjoy the experience?

Related: Agriculture and Dairy Farming, page
Energy Production, page 40
Manufacturing and Mining, page 42

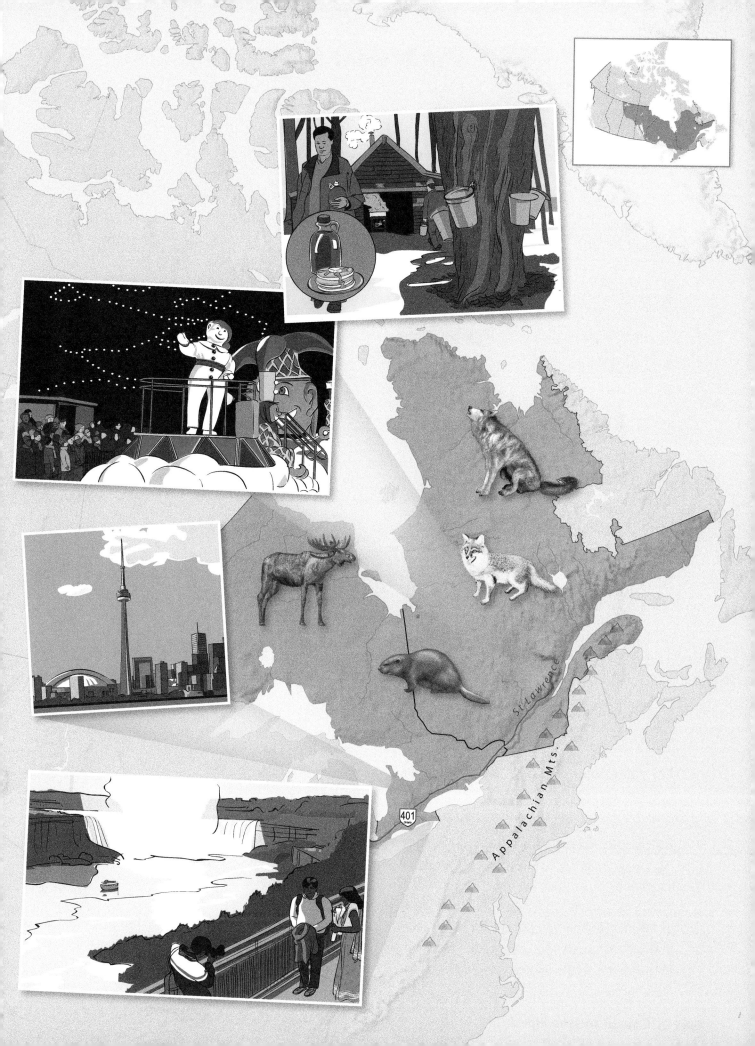

Atlantic and Northern Canada

1. Atlantic and Gulf Region

2. Gulf of St. Lawrence

3. Bay of Fundy

4. Northumberland Strait

5. Grand Banks

6. iceberg

7. Confederation Bridge

8. fishing boat

9. Anne of Green Gables

10. char

11. arctic

12. sub-arctic

13. Mackenzie River

14. tundra

15. northern lights

16. whalebone carvings

17. polar bear

18. snowy owl

Talk about Atlantic Canada and Northern Canada

📱 Use *you can see* to talk about things you find in a location.

In Atlantic Canada, <u>you can see</u> the Confederation Bridge.

In Atlantic Canada, <u>you can see</u> fishing boats.

In Northern Canada, <u>you can see</u> the northern lights.

In Northern Canada, <u>you can see</u> a polar bear.

👥 Look at the pictures. Talk about Atlantic Canada and Northern Canada.

Examples:

In Atlantic Canada, you can see the Grand Banks.

In Northern Canada, you can see snowy owls.

Related: Fisheries, page 36
Manufacturing and Mining, page 4

Atlantic Canada

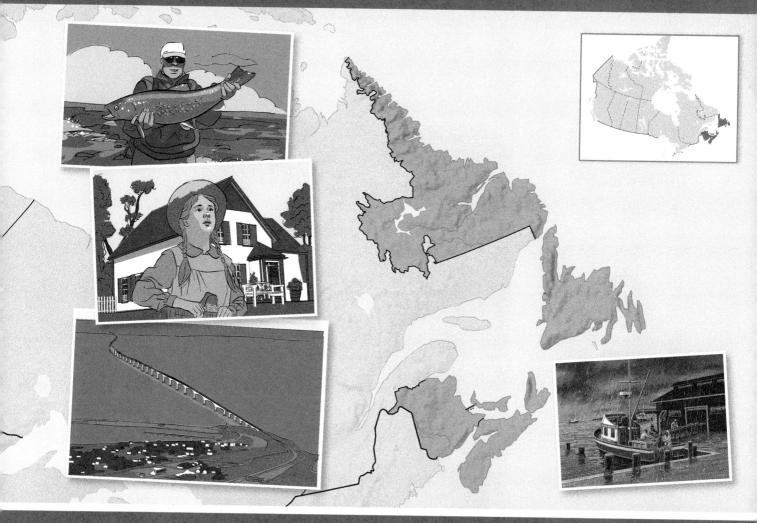

Northern Canada

Forestry

1. forest   **2.** logging   **3.** logger   **4.** chainsaw

  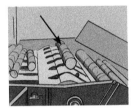 

5. grapple-yarder   **6.** clear-cutting   **7.** wood   **8.** lumber

  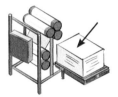 

9. paper mill   **10.** pulp   **11.** paper   **12.** import

13. export

Forestry Stewardship Council

The Forestry Stewardship Council (FSC) was started in 1993 in Toronto, Ontario. People from environmental groups, the forestry industry, aboriginal organizations, and community forestry groups got together because they were upset about the number of trees being cut down. They created a system to show which wood and paper come from responsibly managed forests. The FSC works to make sure natural forests are preserved, that no pesticides are used, and that the rights of aboriginal peoples and forestry workers are maintained. Their logo can be found on any paper or wood product that meets their standards. This allows consumers to know which products are best for the preservation of the world's forests.

Fisheries

1. boat

2. net

3. aquaculture

4. fish farm

5. oyster farm

6. cannery

7. processing plant

8. cod

9. salmon

10. lobster

Aquaculture

Aquaculture is the farming of fish and other freshwater or saltwater creatures. Fish are raised under special conditions, and they are usually sold once they are large enough. In Canada, aquaculture includes fish farms and oyster farms.

This is different from commercial fishing, where wild fish have to be caught using boats and nets. Together, aquaculture and commercial fishing make up the fisheries industry in Canada.

Agriculture and Dairy Farming

1. dairy barn

2. farmer

3. cattle

4. milk

5. dairy

6. hay

7. wheat

8. corn

9. canola

10. kernel

11. grain

12. oil

13. plow

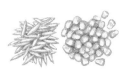

14. harvest

15. combine

16. grain evelator

17. miller

18. grind

19. flour

Count More Than One

 Some nouns cannot be counted.

Farmers plant <u>corn</u>.

Farmers harvest <u>wheat</u>.

Dairy farmers feed <u>cattle</u>.

👥 **Look at the pictures. Talk about agriculture.**

Examples:

Farmers gather hay.

Millers grind wheat into flour.

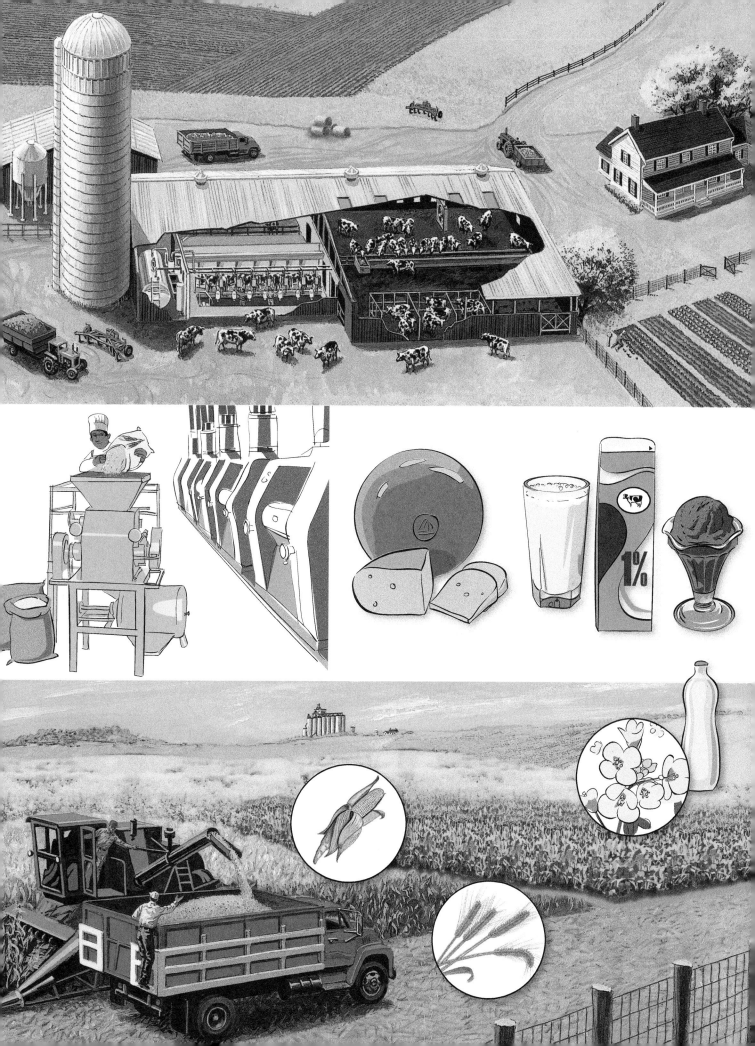

Energy Production

1. hydroelectricity

2. reservoir

3. dam

4. power lines

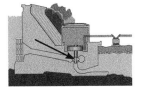
5. turbine

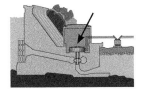
6. generator

7. transformer

8. oil sands

9. oil

10. derrick

11. drill

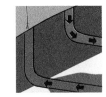
12. wells

13. natural gas

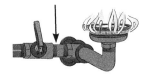
14. pipe

15. pipelines

16. nuclear energy

17. coal

Use a T-chart

Use a T-chart to organize information and ideas.

Tools	Resources
drill	oil
pipelines	natural gas
derrick	water

Look at the T-chart and the pictures. Talk about the resources.

Examples:

People use wells to get oil or natural gas.

People use reservoirs to collect water.

Related: Energy and Electricity, page 14

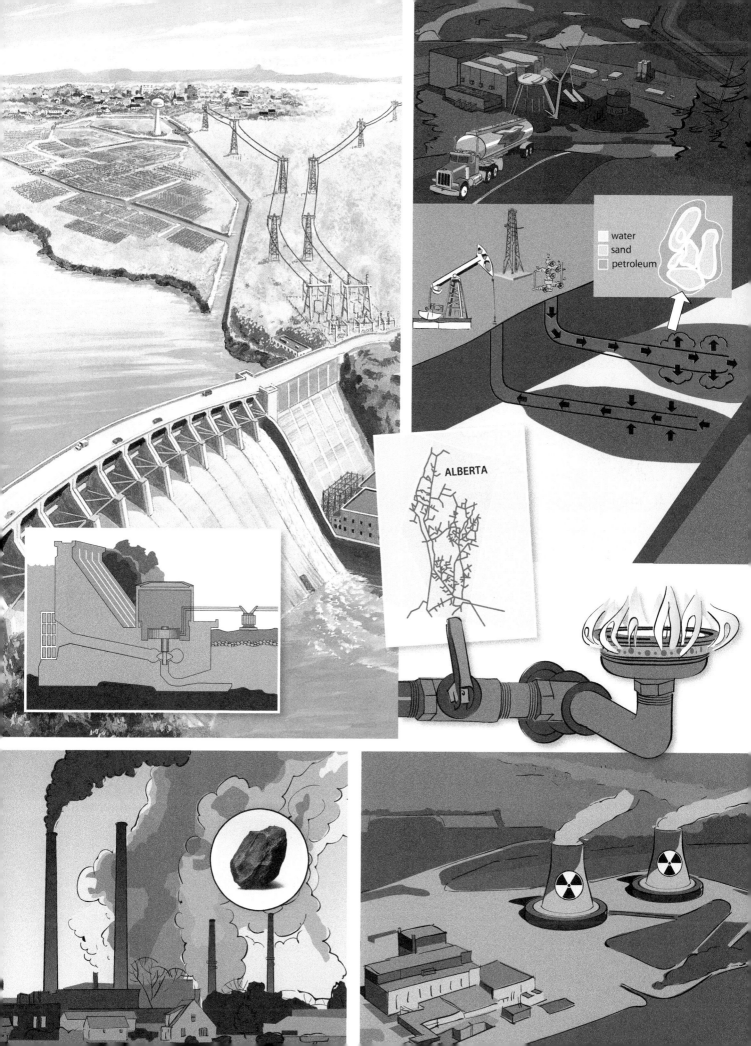

water
sand
petroleum

ALBERTA

Manufacturing and Mining

1. research

2. robotics

3. auto maker

4. software

5. Canadarm

6. products

7. mine

8. shaft

9. potash

10. salt

11. gold

12. diamond

13. copper

14. zinc

15. uranium

16. iron

17. mineral

18. ore

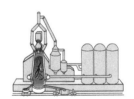

19. smelter

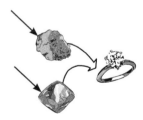

20. raw materials

Mining in Canada

Mining is a major industry in Canada, just like agriculture, forestry, and fisheries. It involves removing valuable rocks and minerals from the earth and turning them into other products. Mining sources cannot be replaced once they have been used. The good news is they can be recycled. Some of these metals and minerals can be reused many times.

Talk about these questions. Make a list of your answers.

What are some things we reuse?

What kinds of things do we recycle?

What kinds of things can we not recycle?

1. European Union

2. Western Europe

3. Iberian peninsula

4. Benelux

5. Scandinavia

6. Central Europe

7. Mediterranean countries

8. Balkan countries

9. Eastern Europe

10. Baltic countries

11. Central Asian Republics

12. Siberia

Talk about Regions

Use *in* to talk about the location of a country.

A: Is Norway <u>in</u> Scandinavia?

B: Yes, Norway is <u>in</u> Scandinavia.

B: Is Romania <u>in</u> Western Europe?

A: No, Romania is <u>in</u> Eastern Europe.

Think of a country. Your partner guesses the country. Take turns.

Example:

A: Is it in Central Europe?

B: Yes, it is.

A: Is it Germany?

B: Yes, it is!

Europe

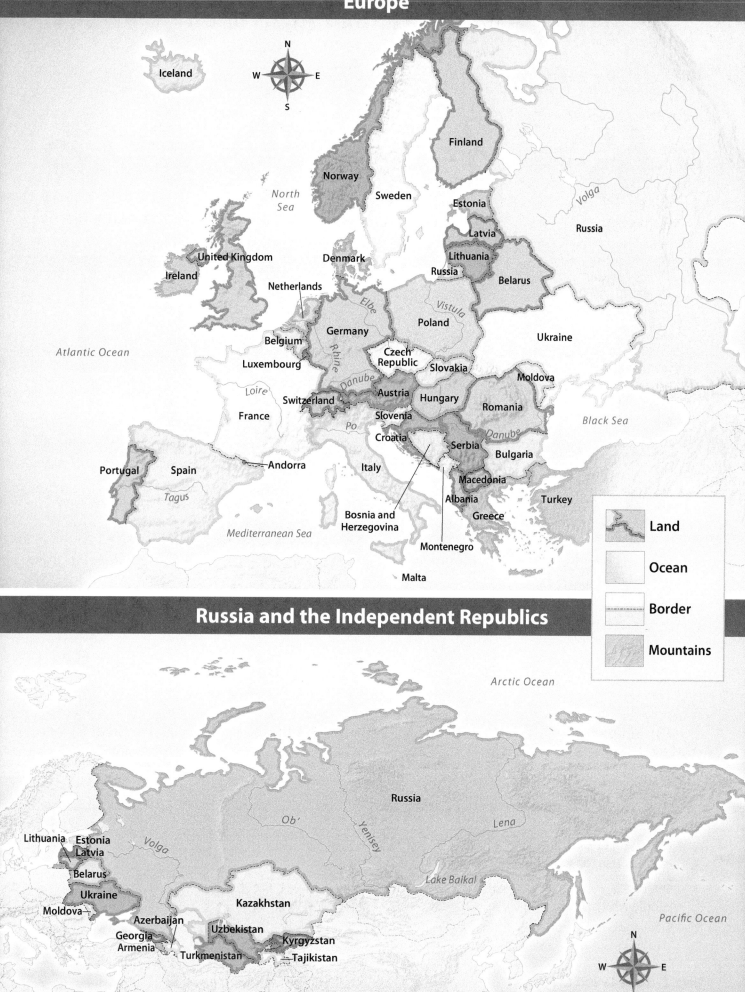

Iceland

N
W   E
S

Norway

North
Sea

Finland

Sweden

Estonia

Volga

Russia

Latvia

Lithuania

United Kingdom

Denmark

Russia

Belarus

Ireland

Netherlands

Elbe

Vistula

Atlantic Ocean

Belgium

Germany

Poland

Ukraine

Luxembourg

Rhine

Czech
Republic

Slovakia

Moldova

Danube

Switzerland

Austria

Hungary

Romania

Loire

France

Po

Slovenia

Black Sea

Croatia

Danube

Portugal

Spain

Andorra

Italy

Serbia

Bulgaria

Tagus

Macedonia

Bosnia and
Herzegovina

Albania

Turkey

Greece

Mediterranean Sea

Montenegro

Malta

	Land
	Ocean
	Border
	Mountains

Russia and the Independent Republics

Arctic Ocean

Russia

Ob'

Yenisey

Lena

Lithuania

Estonia

Latvia

Volga

Belarus

Ukraine

Lake Baikal

Moldova

Kazakhstan

Pacific Ocean

Azerbaijan

Georgia

Uzbekistan

Armenia

Kyrgyzstan

Turkmenistan

Tajikistan

N
W   E
S

Asia, Africa, and Australia
Religions and Important Features

1. Taoism

2. Confucianism

3. Sikhism

4. Hinduism

5. Buddhism

6. Shinto

7. Islam

8. Christianity

9. Judaism

10. Mount Everest

11. Nile River

12. Great Pyramid

13. Sahara

14. Victoria Falls

15. Uluru

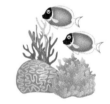

16. Great Barrier Reef

Religions

The map shows where many religions started. When you talk about people who belong to a religion, use the word *practise*.

Examples:

People who practise Judaism are called Jewish.

Many Indonesians practise Islam.

What do you know about these religions? Choose one religion and research it online. Tell a partner what you find out.

Asia

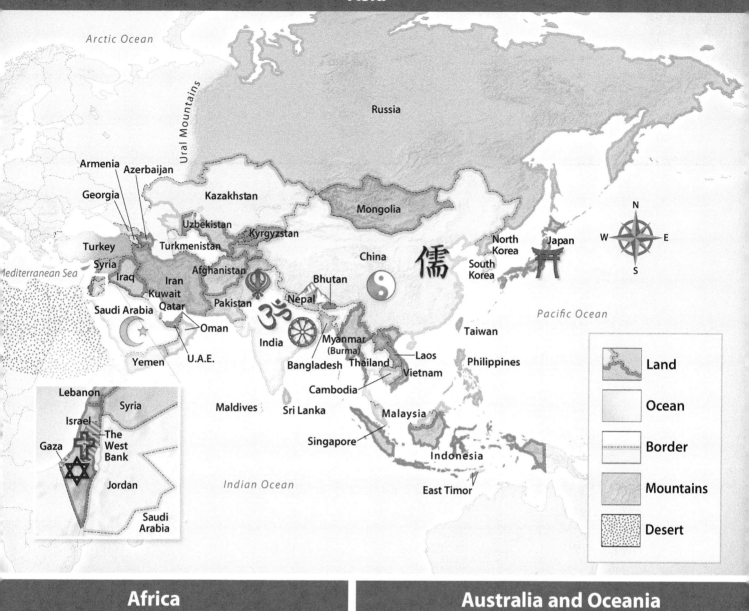

Arctic Ocean

Ural Mountains

Russia

Mediterranean Sea

Armenia
Azerbaijan
Georgia
Kazakhstan
Uzbekistan
Kyrgyzstan
Mongolia
North Korea
Japan
South Korea
Turkey
Turkmenistan
China
Syria
Afghanistan
Iraq
Iran
Bhutan
Kuwait
Pakistan
Nepal
Qatar
Saudi Arabia
Oman
India
Myanmar (Burma)
Laos
Taiwan
Yemen
U.A.E.
Bangladesh
Thailand
Vietnam
Philippines
Cambodia
Maldives
Sri Lanka
Malaysia
Singapore
Indonesia
East Timor

Pacific Ocean

Indian Ocean

N
W E
S

Lebanon
Syria
Israel
The West Bank
Gaza
Jordan
Saudi Arabia

	Land
	Ocean
	Border
	Mountains
	Desert

Africa

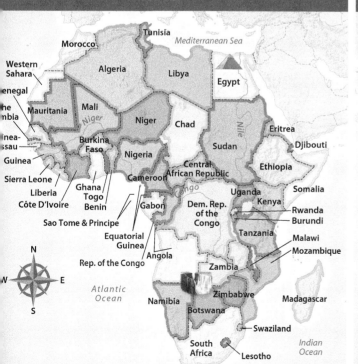

Morocco
Tunisia
Mediterranean Sea
Western Sahara
Algeria
Libya
Egypt
Senegal
Mauritania
Mali
Niger
Chad
Nile
Eritrea
The Gambia
Niger
Sudan
Djibouti
Guinea-Bissau
Burkina Faso
Nigeria
Central African Republic
Ethiopia
Guinea
Sierra Leone
Ghana
Cameroon
Uganda
Somalia
Liberia
Togo
Benin
Gabon
Dem. Rep. of the Congo
Kenya
Côte D'Ivoire
Congo
Rwanda
Burundi
Sao Tome & Principe
Tanzania
Malawi
Equatorial Guinea
Mozambique
Rep. of the Congo
Angola
Zambia
Namibia
Zimbabwe
Madagascar
Botswana
Swaziland
South Africa
Lesotho
Atlantic Ocean
Indian Ocean

N
W E
S

Australia and Oceania

Papua New Guinea
Solomon Islands
Indian Ocean
Vanuatu
Fiji
New Caledonia
Australia
Pacific Ocean
New Zealand
Indian Ocean
Tasman Sea

N
W E
S

The Americas

 1. coffee

 2. chocolate

 **3.** peanuts

 **4.** corn

 5. bananas

 6. oranges

 7. potatoes

 8. rubber

 **9.** vanilla

 10. pumpkins

 11. rice

 12. flowers

 **13.** papayas

 14. cotton

 15. sugar cane

 16. soybeans

Think about the Topic

Look at the map of the Americas. Make a chart of the crops grown here.

Check off the things that you use or eat often. Are most of the crops that you use grown in Canada? If not, how far do these crops travel to get to you?

Crop	Things I Use or Eat

A Canadian Resources T-chart

Look at the T-chart. Check pages 24–49 to find words you don't know.

Natural Resources	Human-made Resources
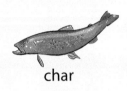 char	 paper mill
wheat	dam
 oil sands	software
 cattle	cannery
 lobster	

B Use Social Studies Skills

👥 **Read the sentences out loud. Point to the pictures in the T-chart.**

A: <u>Wheat</u> is a natural resource.

B: A <u>cannery</u> is a human-made resource.

A: A <u>dam</u> is a human-made resource.

B: <u>Cattle</u> are a natural resource.

A: <u>Software</u> is a human-made resource.

B: <u>Lobster</u> is a natural resource.

C Talk about It

👥 **Ask and answer questions about the T-chart. Keep going.**

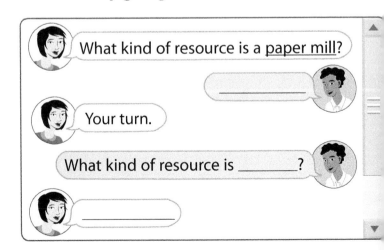

What kind of resource is a <u>paper mill</u>?

_____

Your turn.

What kind of resource is _____?

_____

D Read about It
Canadian Resources

Canada has many resources. The oil sands in Alberta are a very important resource. Canada has a lot of wheat, too. There are also char, cattle, and lobster in Canada. These are all natural resources.

Canada has a lot of human-made resources. It has dams, paper mills, and canneries.

A new Canadian resource is technology. This is a human-made resource. Companies design and create software for computers and phones.

All of these resources are very important in Canada.

E Check Your Understanding

Read the sentences. Are they *true* or *false*?

1. Canada has many natural resources. _T_
2. Canada's oil sands are not very important. ___
3. Canada has a lot of wheat. ___
4. There is char in Canada. ___
5. Canada doesn't have human-made resources. ___
6. There are paper mills in Canada. ___
7. Dams are natural resources. ___
8. Technology is an old resource in Canada. ___

F Write about It

1. Complete a T-chart about resources in your province or territory.

2. Look online to find more resources in your province or territory. Add them to your T-chart.

3. Use the information in your T-chart. Write about your province or territory.

Example:

I live in Nova Scotia. My province has many resources. Lobster, fish, and oysters are important natural resources ...

G Think about It

👥 **Talk with your class. Answer the questions.**

1. **Classify.** Name a resource. Ask your classmates: Is _____ a natural resource or a human-made resource?

2. **Make associations.** Name some natural resources that are important for farming.

3. **Understand cause and effect.** Why is water an important natural resource? What problems can happen if we run out of water?

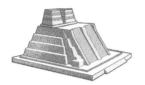

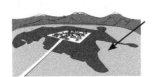

1. Tenochtitlán

2. Lake Texcoco

3. Hernando Cortés

4. Montezuma

5. corn/maize

6. tortilla

7. solar calendar

8. Chichén Itzá

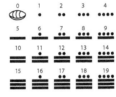

9. pottery

10. stelae

11. mathematics

12. pyramid

13. priests

14. astronomy

15. Machu Picchu

16. Francisco Pizarro

17. Atahualpa

18. terrace farming

19. statues

Ask about the Past

Use *was* and *were* to talk about people and places in the past.

Who <u>was</u> Atahualpa?

Atahualpa <u>was</u> an Incan emperor.

What <u>were</u> stelae?

Stelae <u>were</u> decorated stone slabs.

Look at the map. Ask and answer questions about the past.

Examples:

What was Tenochtitlán?

Who were Hernando Cortés and Francisco Pizarro?

Mexico

Gulf of Mexico

Cuba

Dominican Republic

Jamaica

Haiti

Puerto Rico

Belize
Honduras
Guatemala
El Salvador
Nicaragua
Costa Rica
Panama

Caribbean Sea

Trinidad and Tobago

Orinoco

Venezuela

Guyana

French Guiana

Suriname

Colombia

Ecuador

Amazon

Peru

Brazil

Bolivia

Paraná

Chile

Paraguay

Pacific Ocean

Uruguay

Argentina

N
W   E
S

Aztec Empire

Mayan Empire

Incan Empire

Ancient Mesopotamia and Ancient Egypt

 1. palace

 2. king

 3. trade

 4. agriculture

 5. scribe

 6. cuneiform script

 7. mudbrick

 8. canal

 9. irrigation

 10. pyramid

 11. monuments

 12. desert

 13. tomb

 14. sarcophagus

 15. treasure

 16. gods

 17. embalm

 18. mummy

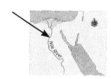 19. pharaoh

 20. slave

 21. papyrus

 22. hieroglyphs

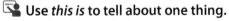 23. Nile

---

Identify What You See

Use *this is* to tell about one thing.

This is a pharaoh.

This is a pyramid.

Use *these are* to talk about more than one thing.

These are scribes.

These are monuments.

Look at the pictures. Talk about ancient Mesopotamia and ancient Egypt.

Examples:

This is the Nile.

These are mudbricks.

Mesopotamia

Tigris River

Euphrates River

The Fertile Crescent

Mediterranean Sea

Lower Egypt

Sinai

Western Desert

Eastern Desert

Red Sea

Upper Egypt

Ancient Greece and Ancient Rome

1. agora

2. column

3. democracy

4. oligarchy

5. monarchy

6. drama

7. Olympic Games

8. Parthenon

9. Acropolis

10. philosophers

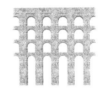

11. consul

12. patrician

13. tribune

14. plebeian

15. aqueduct

16. Colosseum

17. gladiator

18. emperor

Talk about the Past

📝 **Add *ed* to many verbs to tell about the past.**
Athletes <u>played</u> in the Olympic games.
People <u>watched</u> the drama.
Philosophers <u>talked</u> about their ideas.

👥 **Look at the pictures. Talk about Greece and Rome in the present and in the past.**
Examples:
People walk in the agora.
People walked in the agora.

Greece

Alexander the Great

Rome

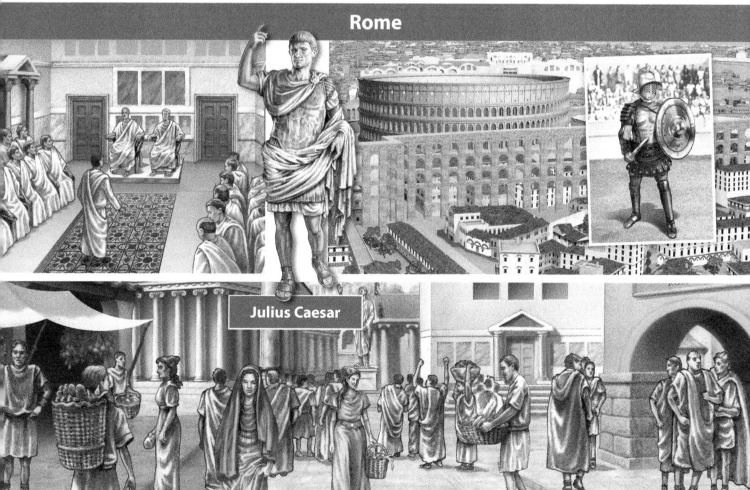

Julius Caesar

Ancient China

1. bronze axe

2. jade

3. lunar calendar

4. Great Wall of China

5. terracotta soldiers

6. emperor

7. terrace farm

8. silk

9. caravan

10. Silk Road

11. fireworks

12. poet

13. woodblock printing

14. Chinese characters

15. compass

16. gunpowder

Think about the Topic

The Silk Road is a name for the paths the ancient Chinese people used to get to other countries. These people travelled along the Silk Road to buy things and to sell items such as silk. They also shared ideas with the people they met along the Silk Road.

Talk about these questions. Make a list of your answers.

Besides silk, what do you think the Chinese people sold on the Silk Road?

What do you think the Chinese people bought from other countries?

Shang Dynasty
18th–11th Century BCE

Qin Dynasty
221–206 BCE

Qin Shi Huangdi

Han Dynasty
206 BCE–220 CE

Tang Dynasty
618–907 CE

Song Dynasty
960–1279 CE

Medieval Europe

1. knight

2. shield

3. helmet

4. sword

5. king

6. queen

7. castle

8. blacksmith

9. royalty

10. nobility

11. peasant

12. monastery

13. monk

14. feudal system

15. Roman Catholic Church

16. crusades

17. moat

18. tailor

19. lord

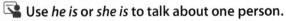
20. lady

21. nun

22. merchant

23. serf

Talk about People

Use *he is* or *she is* to talk about one person.

<u>He is</u> a knight.

<u>She is</u> a nun.

Use *they are* to talk about more than one person.

<u>They are</u> merchants.

<u>They are</u> serfs.

Look at the pictures. Talk about the people.

Examples:

He is a blacksmith.

They are tailors.

Unit 3 World History

Unit 3 Expansion World History

A Achievements in History Chart

Look at the chart. Check pages 52–61 to find words you don't know.

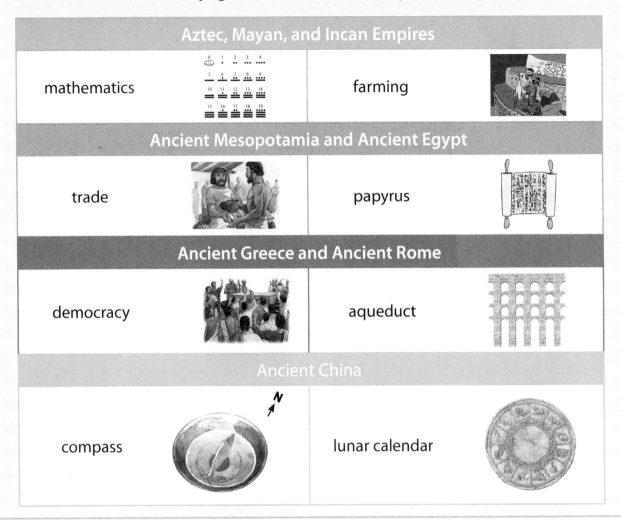

Aztec, Mayan, and Incan Empires	
mathematics	farming

Ancient Mesopotamia and Ancient Egypt	
trade	papyrus

Ancient Greece and Ancient Rome	
democracy	aqueduct

Ancient China	
compass	lunar calendar

B Use Social Studies Skills

👥 Read the sentences out loud. Point to the pictures in the chart.

A: The Mayans created a system of <u>mathematics</u>.

B: The Ancient Romans built thousands of kilometres of <u>aqueducts</u>.

A: The <u>compass</u> was invented in Ancient China.

B: Ancient Mesopotamians developed <u>trade</u> so they could get the things they needed.

C Talk about It

👥 Talk about the chart. Keep going.

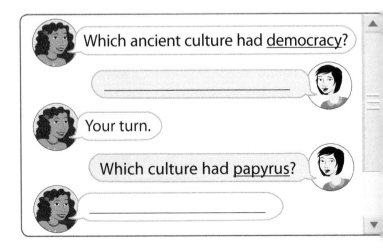

Which ancient culture had <u>democracy</u>?

_____

Your turn.

Which culture had <u>papyrus</u>?

_____

D Read about It

ACHIEVEMENTS IN HISTORY

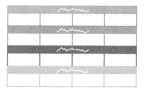

There have been many important achievements throughout history.

The Incas of Peru invented a way to grow crops on the steep mountainside in the Andes. They came up with the idea of terrace farming, or carving steps into the side of the mountain. This idea was so good that some people still use terrace farms today.

The Mesopotamians developed a system of trade to get the items they needed. They learned that they could get things like woods and metals by trading what they had (like textiles) with their neighbours.

The Romans built aqueducts to deliver clean water to people. Some aqueducts were hundreds of miles long and most of them were underground. The way they worked 2000 years ago was similar to the way our plumbing works today.

These achievements happened a long time ago and far from where we live. In some way, however, they all affect how we do things in Canada today.

E Check Your Understanding

Read the sentences. Are they _true_ or _false_?

1. The Incas created a system of trade. _F_

2. Some people still use terrace farms today. ___

3. Mesopotamians traded with their neighbours. ___

4. None of the Roman aqueducts were underground. ___

F Write about It

1. Complete an Achievements in History chart.

2. Look online and in your dictionary to find more information about achievements in history. Put the information into your chart.

3. Use the information from your chart. Write about achievements in history.

> Example:
>
> The Ancient Greeks had a system of democracy ...

G Think about It

👥 **Talk with your class. Answer the questions.**

1. **Identify.** Name some buildings that ancient people built. Ask your classmates: Where was _____ built?

2. **Compare and contrast.** How were ancient Greece and Ancient China different? How were they similar?

3. **Apply.** Imagine you live in the Roman Empire. Describe your life. What do you do every day?

First Nations, Inuit, and Métis History I

 **1.** trap

 **2.** bannock

 **3.** bison hunt

 **4.** pemmican

 **5.** harpoon

 **6.** copper knife

 **7.** log canoe

 **8.** birch bark canoe

 **9.** snowshoe

 **10.** toboggan

 **11.** kayak

 **12.** hide

 **13.** snare

 **14.** Red River cart

 **15.** Louis Riel

 **16.** Red River Rebellion

Talk about the Topic

Bannock is a kind of bread that was eaten by early settlers, fur traders, and some Native peoples. It looks like a round cake or pancake and is usually made with flour, lard, salt, and water. Pemmican is made out of dried meat that is pounded into tiny pieces and mixed with melted fat. This food was popular with fur traders—and the First Nations people from whom they learned about it—because it could be packed and stored for long periods of time.

Talk about these questions. Make a list of your answers.

What are some traditional foods from your culture?

What are some of your favourite foods?

MANITOBA ACT, 1870

33 Victoria, c 3 (Canada)

(AN ACT TO AMEND AND CONTINUE THE ACT 32 AND 33
VICTORIA CHAPTER 3; AND TO ESTABLISH AND PROVIDE FOR
THE GOVERNMENT OF THE PROVINCE OF MANITOBA)

WHEREAS it is probable that Her Majesty The Queen may, pursuant to the
Constitution Act, 1867, be pleased to admit Rupert's Land and the North-Western
Territory into the Union or Dominion of Canada, before the next Session of the
Parliament of Canada:

And Whereas it is expedient to prepare for the transfer of the said Territories to the
Government of Canada at the time appointed by the Queen for such admission:

And Whereas it is expedient also to provide for the organization of part of the said
Territories as a Province, and for the establishment of a Government therefor, and to
make provision for the Civil Government of the remaining part of the said Territories,
not included within ...

THE LIST OF RIGHTS

as Drawn by the Executive of the Provisional Government

I. That the Territories heretofore known as Rupert's Land and North-West, shall not
enter into the Confederation of the Dominion of Canada, except as a Province, to be
styled and known as the Province of Assiniboia, and with all the rights and privileges
common to the different Provinces of the Dominion.

II. That we have two Representatives in the Senate, and four in the House of Commons
of Canada, until such time as an increase of population entitle this Province to a greater
Representation.

III. That the Province of Assiniboia shall not be held liable at any time for any portion
of the Public debt of the Dominion contracted before the date the said Province shall
have first received from ... ... for which the said Province is to be held liable.

... ... Thousand ($80,000) dollars be paid annually by the Dominion

... ... the local Legislature of this Province.

V. That all properties, rights and privileges enjoyed [sic: enjoyed] by the people of this
Province, up to the date of our entering into this Confederation, be respected; and that
the arrangement and confirmation of all customs, usages and privileges be left
exclusively to the local Legislature.

VI. That during the term of five years, the Province of Assiniboia shall not be subjected
to any direct taxation, except such as may be imposed by local Legislature, for
municipal or local purposes.

VII. That a sum of money equal to eighty cents per head of the population of this
Province, be paid annually by the Canadian Government to the local Legislature of the

First Nations, Inuit, and Métis History II

1. powwow

2. rock painting

3. longhouse

4. weave

5. totem pole

6. mask

7. teepee

8. crest

9. bark lodge

10. wigwam

11. inuksuk

12. igloo

13. carve

14. elders

15. chief

16. Six Nations Confederacy

17. stockade

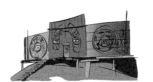

18. plank house

Six Nations Confederacy

The Six Nations Confederacy began as the League of Five Nations, also called the League of the Iroquois. This was an alliance between five First Nations originally located in northern New York state—the Seneca, Cayuga, Oneida, Onondaga, and Mohawk.

When the Tuscarora joined the confederacy in the early 18th century, the group became known as the Six Nations and are sometimes referred to as the Haudenosaunee or the Iroquois. They now live in parts of Ontario, Quebec, and some US states.

Na-Dene

Tsimshian

Wakashan

Salish

Kutenai

Siouan

Eskaleut

Algonquian

Iroquoian

European Explorers

1. Leif Ericsson

2. Vikings

3. John Cabot

4. Jacques Cartier

5. Donnacona

6. Samuel de Champlain

7. Henry Hudson

8. colonialism

9. colony

10. New France

11. mercantilism

12. route

13. Northwest Passage

14. ship

15. sail

16. sea astrolabe

Think about the Topic

Mercantilism is the idea that there is always a fixed amount of wealth in the world. A country has to export more goods than it imports in order to gain wealth. From the 17th to 19th centuries, countries like England and France sent explorers to look for new sources of raw materials in the Americas. They could take control of these raw materials and export them to other countries in order to make more money.

Can you think of some things exported from Canada? What do we have to import? Create a chart.

Imports	Exports

Leif Ericsson, Circa 1000

John Cabot, 1497

Jacques Cartier, 1534

Jacques Cartier, 1535–36

Northwest Passage

Hudson's 1610–11 route

Hudson's 1609 route

Arctic Circle

Hudson River

Champlain, 1615–16   Champlain 1609–13

Champlain, 1604–07

Birth of a Nation

 1. Charlottetown Conference

 2. Fathers of Confederation

 3. confederation

 4. constitution

 5. habitation

 6. homestead

 7. log cabin

 8. seigneury

 9. Hurons

 10. Jesuits

 11. missionary

 12. priest

 13. plow

 14. tradesperson

 15. blacksmith

16. miller

 17. cooper

 18. peddler

 19. storekeeper

 20. merchant

The Charlottetown Conference

The Charlottetown Conference took place in Charlottetown, PEI, from September 1 to September 9, 1864. Representatives from the Province of Canada, New Brunswick, Nova Scotia, and Prince Edward Island met to discuss a union between all members of British North America. They created a plan that would lead to the British North America Act and Canada's confederation in 1867.

Think about what you know about confederation. Create a KWL chart. Fill it in as you learn more.

What I Know	What I Want to Know	What I Learned

Unit 4   Canadian History

New France, 17th Century

...dia and New France, 1700

British North America, 1791

Canada, 1867

Farm divided among several married children

River

The Fur Trade

1. trading posts

2. beaver

3. beaver pelt

4. beaver hat

5. furs

6. barter

7. Étienne Brûlé

8. coureurs de bois

9. voyageurs

10. rapids

11. portage

12. moccasins

Write about the Past

Some verbs do not end in *ed* in the past.

build   ⟶   built
have   ⟶   had
ride   ⟶   rode
wear   ⟶   wore
make   ⟶   made

Look at the pictures. Write about what you see

Examples:

The first Métis people had one Aboriginal parent and one parent who was a European fur trader.

The traders built trading posts.

They made furs into clothing.

Hudson's Bay Company.

1610 →

Hudson's Bay Company.

1681 →

Battle of the Plains of Abraham (1759) and War of 1812

 1. Major-General Louis-Joseph de Montcalm

 2. Major-General James Wolfe

 3. French

 **4.** British

 5. redcoats

 **6.** conflicts

 **7.** fortifications

 **8.** musket

 **9.** Battle of Queenston Heights

 **10.** Tecumseh

 11. Major-General Isaac Brock

 **12.** Major-General Roger Hale Sheaffe

 13. military/troops

 14. soldier

 15. militia

 16. Laura Secord

 **17.** treaty

 18. allies

 **19.** privateers

 20. cannon

The Treaty of Ghent

On June 18, 1812, the United States declared war on Great Britain. At the time, Canada was part of Great Britain. The British fought with the Canadians and their First Nations allies against the Americans, but the two sides were too evenly matched. Neither side could win the war.

On Christmas Eve in 1814, the United States and Great Britain agreed to sign the Treaty of Ghent. This document ended the war and both countries agreed to return any captured territory. Things returned to the way they were before the war started.

Battle of the Plains of Abraham (1759)

War of 1812

Battle of Queenston Heights

Treaty of Ghent

Canadian Pacific Railway

 1. Sandford Fleming

 2. William Cornelius Van Horne

 3. navvy/ labourer

 4. engineer

 5. surveyor

 6. pack horses

 7. navvy camp

 8. track

 9. rail

10. spike

11. tie

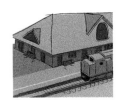 12. station

 13. blast/explosion

14. dynamite

15. tunnel

16. landslide

The Canadian Pacific Railway

In 1881, the Canadian Pacific Railway began construction to expand the railway from Ontario to British Columbia. William Cornelius Van Horne was in charge of making sure this happened quickly. Thousands of navvies were hired to work on the railway. Many of the workers in British Columbia were from China.

They were paid less money than the other workers and were given more dangerous jobs. Without their help, construction of the railway would not have been completed. The railway was completed in 1885. In 2006, the Canadian government offered an apology to the Chinese population for the treatment of the workers during construction of the railway.

Kamloops
Edmonton
Port Moody
Battleford
Kicking
Horse Pass
Calgary
Regina
Moose Jaw
Brandon
Selkirk
Rat Portage (Kenora)
Winnipeg
Fort William
Lake
Nipissing

CP Rail
CP Rail
CP Rail

Gold Rush and Development of Western Canada

1. steamer

2. prairie town

3. prospector

4. claim

5. claim post

6. sift

7. pan

8. rocker

9. gold

10. nugget

11. tent

12. Martha Louise Black

13. mine

14. shack

Martha Louise Black

Martha Louise Black was born in Chicago in 1866. In 1898, she decided to join the Gold Rush and travelled to the Yukon. She opened a milling business there a few years later. She married George Black, who represented the Yukon in parliament for many years. During this time, Martha actively supported the Yukon and the people who lived there.

When her husband was not able to run for parliament in 1935, Martha decided to run for his spot. At the age of 70, she campaigned across the territory, often travelling from place to place on foot! She won the election and became the second woman ever to be elected to Canadian Parliament.

Arctic Ocean

U.S.A

CANADA

Yukon Territory

Yukon River

Dawson City

Whitehorse

Dyea

Skagway

Juneau

Gulf of Alaska

All Canada Route

Skagway/Dyea Route

All Water Route

Edmonton

Pacific Ocean

Vancouver

Seattle

Women's Suffrage Movement

1. temperance

2. prohibition

3. vote

4. petition

5. demonstration

6. rights

7. discrimination

8. protest

9. equality

10. Famous Five

11. Nellie McClung

12. Emily Murphy

13. Henrietta Muir Edwards

14. Louise McKinney

15. Irene Parlby

16. Dr. Emily Howard Stowe

The Famous Five

The Famous Five were a group of women who worked to improve women's rights in Canada. Led by Emily Murphy, the group included Henrietta Muir Edwards, Nellie McClung, Louise McKinney, and Irene Parlby. They participated in various movements for women's rights, including a nationwide campaign for women's suffrage. Most famously, they were involved with the Persons Case, which was heard by the Supreme Court of Canada. The Famous Five fought so women could hold public office as Canadian senators. In 1928 the Supreme Court ruled against the case, but the decision was reversed in 1929 by the British Privy Council and women were allowed to become senators.

A Canadian History Timeline

Look at the timeline. Check pages 64–81 to find words you don't know.

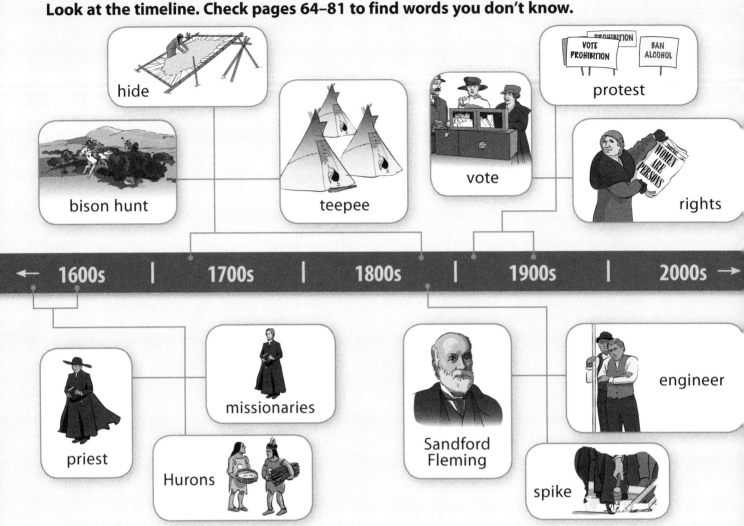

hide

bison hunt

teepee

vote

protest

rights

← 1600s | 1700s | 1800s | 1900s | 2000s →

priest

missionaries

Hurons

Sandford Fleming

engineer

spike

B Use Social Studies Skills

**Read the sentences out loud.
Point to the pictures on the timeline.**

A: <u>Sandford Fleming</u> was an <u>engineer</u>.

B: The <u>bison hunt</u> was an important part of some First Nations cultures.

A: Women were allowed to <u>vote</u> in federal elections after 1918.

B: <u>Missionaries</u> in New France tried to make the <u>Hurons</u> follow a new religion.

C Talk about It

Ask and answer questions about the timeline. Keep going.

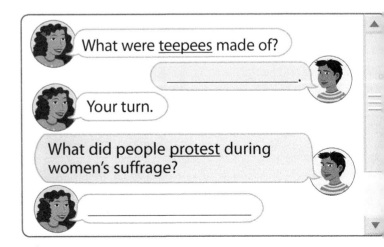

What were <u>teepees</u> made of?

_____.

Your turn.

What did people <u>protest</u> during women's suffrage?

_____

D Read about It

Canadian History

Many events are important to Canadian history. Jesuit missionaries came to New France during the 17th century. They wanted the Hurons to become Catholic. These priests and other missionaries were explorers, too. They were the first Europeans to see many parts of Canada.

The bison hunt was important to the First Nations peoples who lived in what are now the Prairies. They used the bison's meat for food, the bones to make tools and weapons, and the hide to make clothing and teepees. Soon after the Europeans came to this area, the bison herds were almost eliminated.

Sandford Fleming was a railway engineer. He wanted to build a railway to connect the eastern part of Canada with the western part. The Canadian government thought this was a good idea. It began building the Canadian Pacific Railway in 1881. Fleming was there when the last spike was driven into the railway in 1885.

Women in Canada could not always vote. They held protests to let the government know this was unfair. In 1918, Canadian women were given the right to vote in federal elections. This was one of many important events in Canadian history.

E Check Your Understanding

Read the sentences. Are they *true* or *false*?

1. Missionaries came to New France in the 18th century. __T__

2. The missionaries were explorers. ___

3. Teepees were made from bison hides. ___

4. The last spike was driven into the Canadian Pacific Railway in 1881. ___

5. Canadian women have always been allowed to vote. ___

F Write about It

1. Make a timeline of the fur trade in Canada.

2. Look online to find more information about the fur trade in Canada. Add the information to your timeline. Be sure to include information about the contributions of Aboriginal peoples.

3. Use the information on your timeline. Write about the fur trade in Canada.

Example:

In 1610, coureurs de bois became involved in the fur trade ...

G Think about It

Talk with your class. Answer the questions.

1. **Describe**. Discuss with your classmates: What was it like to be a woman at the beginning of the 19th century?

2. **Understand cause and effect**. Why were the bison herds almost eliminated after the Europeans arrived? What effect do you think this had on the First Nations peoples?

3. **Make connections.** Sandford Fleming had a big idea. He wanted to build a railway across Canada. Think about a time you had a big idea. What was your idea? Was your idea a success?

Canadian Government

1. parliament buildings

2. Peace Tower

3. parliament

4. prime minister

5. cabinet

6. House of Commons

7. member of parliament

8. senate

9. senator

10. Governor General

11. mace

12. political parties

13. election

14. candidates

15. voter/elector

16. polling stations

17. ballot

18. premier

19. mayor

20. federal

21. provincial

22. municipal

23. self-government

24. aboriginal

25. elder

26. chief

Make Different Kinds of Sentences

The person who does the action can come before the action word.

The voters elect members of parliament.

The person who does the action can come after the action word, too.

Members of parliament are elected by the voters.

Look at the pictures. Talk about what you see.
Examples:
The senate is appointed by the Governor General.
The premier leads the provincial government.

BLOC QUÉBÉCOIS

NDP

Liberal

Ballots

ALLARD, Marie
APPIAH, Kofi
JOHNSON, Sylvie
URBONAS, Peter

CITY OF VICTORIA

Victoria

New Brunswick

People in Canadian History

1. John A. Macdonald
1815–1891

2. Alexander Mackenzie
1822–1892

3. Wilfrid Laurier
1841–1919

4. William Lyon
Mackenzie King
1874–1950

5. Lester B. Pearson
1897–1972

6. Pierre Elliott Trudeau
1919–2000

7. Kim Campbell
1947–

8. Louis de Baude,
Comte de Frontenac
1622–1698

9. John Graves Simcoe
1752–1806

10. Louis–Joseph
Papineau 1786–1871

11. Francis Bond Head
1793–1875

12. Robert Baldwin
1804–1858

13. Louis–Hippolyte
LaFontaine
1807–1864

14. George–Étienne
Cartier
1814–1873

15. Emily Carr
1871–1945

16. Agnes Macphail
1890–1954

17. Frederick
Banting
1891–1941

18. Tommy
Douglas
1904–1986

19. Roberta
Bondar
1945–

20. Terry Fox
1958–1981

21. Wayne
Gretzky
1961–

Talk about Important Dates

Use *in* + the year to talk about important dates
in history.

Tommy Douglas was born <u>in 1904</u>.

Emily Carr died <u>in 1945</u>.

Terry Fox ran the Marathon of Hope <u>in 1980</u>.

Pierre Elliott Trudeau became prime minister of Canada <u>in 1968</u>.

Look at the pictures. Talk about
important dates.

Examples:

John A. Macdonald was born in 1815.

Kim Campbell became prime minister in 1993.

Immigration and Multiculturalism

1. immigrants

2. refugees

3. war

4. famine

5. citizenship

6. rights

7. responsibilities

8. diversity

9. tradition

10. culture

11. community

12. Clifford Sifton

Clifford Sifton

Clifford Sifton was Prime Minister Wilfrid Laurier's Minister of the Interior. This means that he was in charge of land management, aboriginal affairs, and natural resources. As Minister of the Interior, he started an immigration policy to get people to settle in the West.

He was trying to increase the population in order to develop more of the land. He got settlers to come from the United States and Europe. These immigrants created successful farms.

The Global Community

1. globalization

2. The Commonwealth

3. Organization of the American States

Asia-Pacific Economic Cooperation

4. Asia-Pacific Economic Cooperation

5. United Nations

6. International Olympic Committee

7. Kyoto Accord

8. activists

9. volunteers

10. UNICEF

11. Red Cross

12. Habitat for Humanity International

Globalization

Globalization is a term used to describe changes in how we deal with different countries around the world. It is getting easier to exchange goods and services across the globe. New technology has made communication with other countries fast and simple. This means that ideas, languages, and popular culture from one country can be easily shared with other countries.

Some people believe globalization is good because it improves trade and communication. Others believe it is a bad thing because some cultures and traditions may be lost.

Can you think of some examples of globalization?

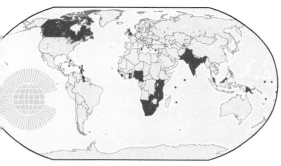

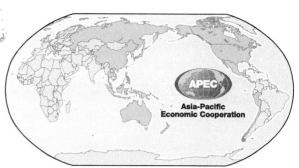

THE UNIVERSAL DECLARATION
OF **Human Rights**

WHEREAS recognition of the inherent dignity and of the equal and inalienable rights of all members of the human family is the foundation of freedom, justice and peace in the world,

WHEREAS disregard and contempt for human rights have resulted in barbarous acts which have outraged the conscience of mankind, and the advent of a world in which human beings shall enjoy freedom of speech and belief and freedom from fear and want has been proclaimed as the highest aspiration of the common people,

Stop Global Warming

ideas technology trade culture

A Important Canadians Fact-and-Opinion Chart

Look at the fact-and-opinion chart. Check pages 84–91 to find words you don't know.

Fact	Opinion
John A. Macdonald was Canada's first prime minister.	John A. Macdonald was Canada's most important prime minister.
The Famous Five worked for women's rights in Canada.	It is important for men and women to have equal rights.
Tommy Douglas introduced universal public healthcare to Canada.	Tommy Douglas made the greatest contribution to Canada.
Wayne Gretzky played hockey for the Edmonton Oilers.	Wayne Gretzky was the best player in the NHL.

B Use Social Skills

👥 **Read the sentences out loud. Point to the pictures in the chart.**

A: John A. Macdonald helped to create Canada.

B: The Famous Five wanted more rights for women.

A: Universal healthcare was introduced by Tommy Douglas.

B: Wayne Gretzky was a hockey player in the NHL.

C Talk about It

👥 **Look at the chart. Take turns asking** *Fact or opinion?* **Keep going.**

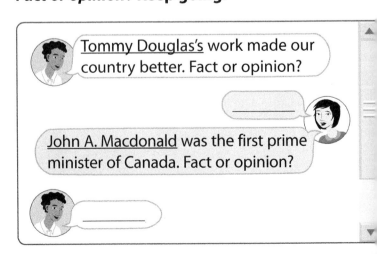

Tommy Douglas's work made our country better. Fact or opinion?

_____

John A. Macdonald was the first prime minister of Canada. Fact or opinion?

_____

D Read about It

Important Canadians

There are many important people in Canada's history. John A. Macdonald was Canada's first prime minister. He was one of the Fathers of Confederation. They created the British North America Act that made Canada a united country in 1867.

The Famous Five were a group of women who wanted to improve women's rights. They helped get Canadian women the right to vote in 1918. They also fought for the right to be appointed to the Canadian Senate.

Tommy Douglas became the premier of Saskatchewan in 1944. He introduced universal public healthcare to Canada. His work is one of the reasons why all Canadians now have healthcare.

Wayne Gretzky was born in Brantford, Ontario. He played hockey in the NHL for the Edmonton Oilers. He helped them win four Stanley Cup championships in five years.

All of these famous Canadians contributed in some way to the history of our country. Many important Canadians have helped to change and improve our country.

E Check Your Understanding

Read the sentences. Are they *true* or *false*?

1. John A. Macdonald was Canada's second prime minister. _T_

2. Women gained the right to vote in 1918. ___

3. Tommy Douglas introduced universal healthcare. ___

4. Wayne Gretzky was born in Edmonton, Alberta. ___

5. Women can be appointed to the Senate. ___

F Write about It

1. Complete a fact-and-opinion chart about an important Canadian.

2. Look online to find more facts about this important Canadian. Add them to your chart. Write your opinion about each fact.

3. Use the information in your chart. Write about an important Canadian.

Example:

Roberta Bondar is an important Canadian. She is important because …

G Think about It

**👥 Talk with your class.
Answer the questions.**

1. **Identify.** With your classmates, discuss three important Canadians. What were their contributions to Canada?

2. **Make inferences.** Why is it important to recognize these people and their contributions?

3. **Draw conclusions.** Why are people like John A. Macdonald and The Famous Five important in our history?

Parts of the Body

 1. head

 2. hair

 3. eye

 4. ear

 5. nose

 6. mouth

 7. teeth

 8. chin

 **9.** neck

 **10.** shoulder

 **11.** arm

 **12.** elbow

 **13.** wrist

 **14.** hand

 **15.** finger

 **16.** thumb

 **17.** chest

 18. leg

 19. knee

 20. ankle

 21. foot

 22. toe

Show Ownership

📝 Use *my* to describe what belongs to you.

This is <u>my</u> eye.

This is <u>my</u> foot.

Use *his* and *her* to describe what belongs to others.

That is <u>his</u> hand. (a boy)

That is <u>her</u> chin. (a girl)

👥 **Look at the picture and yourselves. Talk about parts of the body.**

Examples:

That is his arm.

This is my foot.

Inside the Human Body

1. skeleton

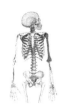

2. bone

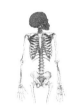

3. skull

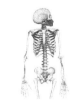

4. jaw

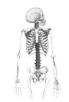

5. spine

6. muscle

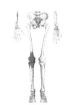

7. joint

8. cartilage

9. ligament

10. tendon

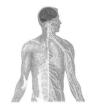

11. brain

12. nerve

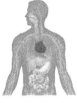

13. heart

14. blood vessels

15. artery

16. vein

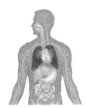

17. lungs

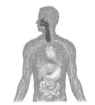

18. esophagus

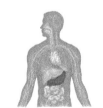

19. stomach

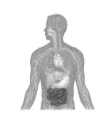

20. intestine

Ask What Body Parts Do

 Use *function* to ask what body parts do.

What is the <u>function</u> of the heart?

The heart pumps blood.

What is the <u>function</u> of the skull?

The skull protects the brain.

Look at the picture. Ask and answer questions about body parts.

Example:

What is the function of the lungs?

The lungs help you breathe.

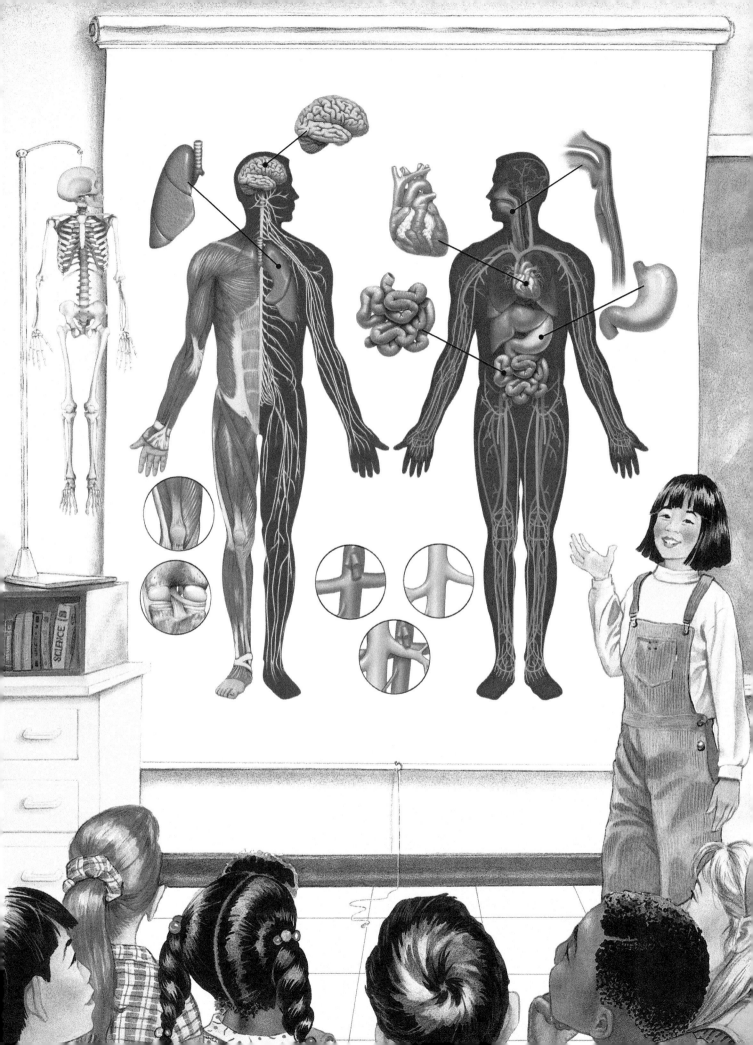

1. sight

2. bright

3. dark

4. hearing

5. loud

6. soft

7. smell

8. fragrant

9. foul

10. taste

11. sweet

12. sour

13. salty

14. touch

15. smooth

16. rough

Give Examples

Use *for example* to support ideas.

Idea: Some things do not taste sweet.

Support: <u>For example</u>, lemons taste sour.

Idea: Some things do not smell good.

Support: <u>For example</u>, trash smells foul.

Write sentences about your senses. Give examples.

Some things are loud.
For example, _____ are loud.
Some things feel _____.
For example, _____

A Body Parts and Senses Fishbone Diagram

Look at the fishbone diagram. Check pages 94–99 to find words you don't know.

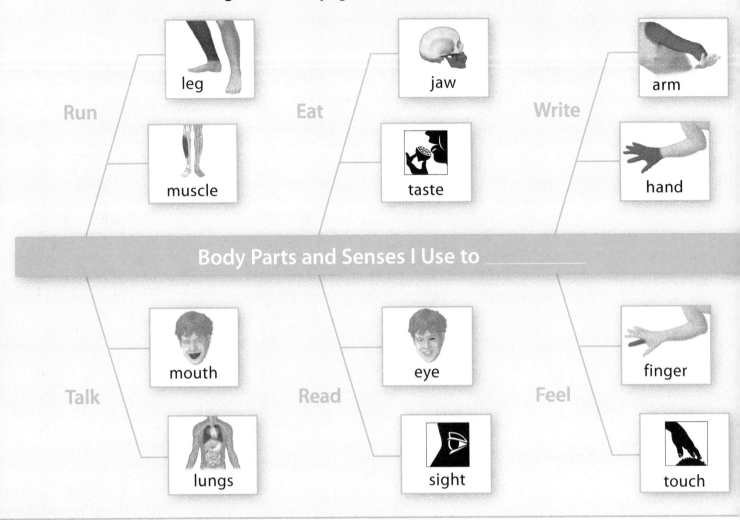

Run — leg, muscle

Eat — jaw, taste

Write — arm, hand

Body Parts and Senses I Use to _____

Talk — mouth, lungs

Read — eye, sight

Feel — finger, touch

B Use Science Skills

👥 **Read the sentences out loud. Point to the pictures in the diagram.**

A: I use my <u>mouth</u> and <u>lungs</u> to talk.

B: I use my <u>eyes</u> and sense of <u>sight</u> to read.

A: I use my <u>legs</u> and <u>muscles</u> to run.

B: I use my <u>jaw</u> and sense of <u>taste</u> to eat.

A: I use my <u>arm</u> and <u>hand</u> to write.

B: I use my <u>finger</u> and sense of <u>touch</u> to feel.

C Talk about It

👥 **Ask and answer questions about the fishbone diagram. Keep going.**

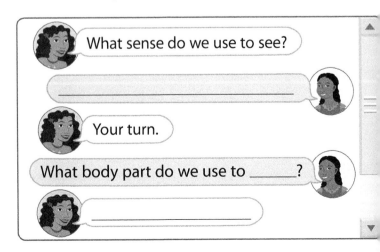

What sense do we use to see?

_____

Your turn.

What body part do we use to _____?

_____

D Read about It

Body Parts and Senses

Our bodies help us do many things. Our senses help us, too.

We use our legs and muscles to run. We use our arms and hands to write. We use our mouths and jaws to eat food. Our esophagus muscles move food to our stomachs. We also use our mouths to talk. We push air from our lungs. We use the air to talk and sing.

We use our senses to do many things. We use our senses of taste and smell to eat. Most of us use our sense of sight to read. People who cannot see can read special books. They use their sense of touch to feel special letters.

We do many things every day. We use parts of our bodies and our senses to do these activities.

E Check Your Understanding

Read the sentences. Are they *true* or *false*?

1. We use our legs and muscles to run. __T__

2. Our lungs help us to eat food. ____

3. Muscles in our legs move food. ____

4. We use our mouths to talk. ____

5. We do not use senses for any activities. ____

6. We use our blood vessels to eat. ____

7. Our sense of smell helps us to read. ____

8. Some people use their sense of touch to read. ____

F Write about It

1. Complete a Body Parts and Senses fishbone diagram.

2. Look in your dictionary to find more body parts and senses. Think about activities that use these parts and senses. Add them to your diagram.

3. Use the information in your diagram. Write about the body parts and senses.

Example:

We use our hands and arms to lift things. We also use our muscles ...

G Think about It

👥 **Talk with your class. Answer the questions.**

1. **Identify.** Name three body parts you use to do homework.

2. **Explain.** Which sense is the most important to you? Why?

3. **Understand cause and effect.** Why is it important to exercise? What happens to your body without exercise?

Exploring Science

1. equipment

2. tape measure

3. forceps

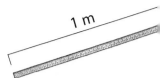

1 m

4. metre stick

5. magnifying glass

6. microscope

7. slide

8. safety glasses

9. graduated cylinder

10. beaker

11. hot plate

FIRST AID

12. first aid kit

13. fire extinguisher

14. diagram

Length	Mass
5.4	10.0
5.8	10.4
6.1	11.3
6.4	11.6
7.7	11.9
9.1	13.2
10.6	13.0
11.5	16.9
12.3	17.7
13.2	18.5

15. chart

Length	Mass
5.4	10.0
5.8	10.4

16. data

17. model

18. triple-beam balance

Use Order Words

Use *first*, *second*, and *third* to talk about steps in a process.

First, gather your equipment.

Second, put on your saftey glasses.

Third, begin your experiment.

Look at the pictures. Write about the steps shown.

Example:
First, design the experiment.

Unit 7 Living Things

Design Experiment

Measure

Observe

Collect Data

Report

Cells and Living Organisms

1. plant cell

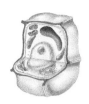

2. cell wall

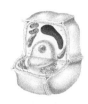

3. vacuole

4. animal cell

5. cell membrane

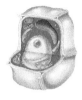

6. cytoplasm

7. nucleus

8. chromosome

9. mitochondrion

10. endoplasmic reticulum

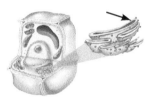

11. ribosome

12. Golgi apparatus

13. seedless plants

14. cone-bearing plants

15. flowering plants

16. monera

17. protists

18. fungi

19. invertebrates

20. vertebrates

Describe Living Organisms

📝 Use *have* to describe plants and animals.

Cells <u>have</u> chromosomes.

Monerans <u>have</u> only one cell.

Many plants <u>have</u> leaves.

Some animals <u>have</u> four legs.

👥 Look at the pictures. Write about cells and living organisms.

Examples:

Many kinds of plants have flowers.

Plants cells have cell walls.

Plants

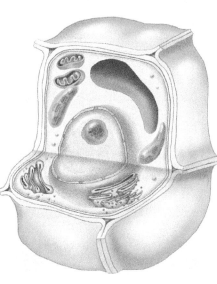

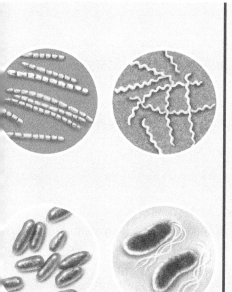
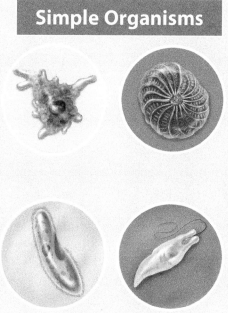
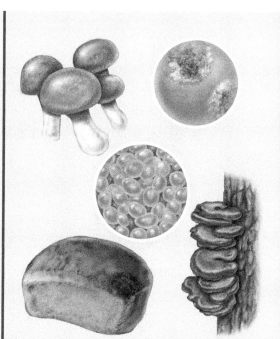

Animals

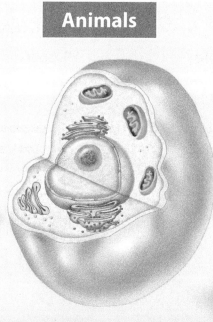

Plants

1. branch

2. needle

3. pine cone

4. nut

5. seed

6. tree

7. trunk

8. limb

9. bark

10. leaf

11. flower

12. petal

13. stamen

14. pistil

15. pollen

16. bud

17. stalk/stem

18. bulb

19. root

Describe Plants

Use *below* and *above* to describe where something is.

The bulb is <u>below</u> the stalk.

The bud is <u>above</u> the stalk.

The trunk is <u>below</u> the branch.

The limb is <u>above</u> the trunk.

above →

below →

Look at the pictures. Talk about what you see.

Examples:

The root is below the stalk.

The flower is above the bulb.

Photosynthesis

1. light energy

2. water

3. cuticle

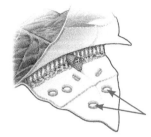

4. stomata

5. carbon dioxide

6. oxygen

7. water vapour

8. transpiration

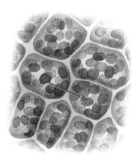

9. chloroplast

10. chlorophyll

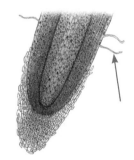

11. root hair

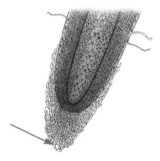

12. root cap

Describe Motion

Use *goes through* to describe how something moves.

Water <u>goes through</u> the dirt.

Water vapour <u>goes through</u> the stomata.

Carbon dioxide <u>goes through</u> the stomata.

Look at the pictures. Talk about what you see.

Examples:

The root cap goes through the dirt.

Light energy goes through the window.

How Do Plants Make **Food?**

glucose

chlorophyll

H_2O

O_2

CO_2

Vegetables

1. lettuce

2. celery

3. cabbage

4. broccoli

5. cauliflower

6. carrot

7. onion

8. radish

9. peppers

10. lima beans

11. cucumber

12. string bean

13. potato

14. yam

15. mushroom

16. peas

Show Similarities

Use a T-chart to put similar things into groups.

Grows above Ground	Grows Underground
cabbage	carrot

Look at the T-chart and the pictures. Talk about vegetables.

A: Cabbage grows above ground.

B: Carrots grow _____.

A: _____ grows _____.

B: _____

Fruit

1. banana

2. pineapple

3. cantaloupe

4. watermelon

5. tomato

6. peach

7. cherry

8. avocado

9. apple

10. pear

11. lemon

12. lime

13. orange

14. grapefruit

15. strawberry

16. raspberry

17. citrus

18. pit

19. section

20. rind

Talk about Where Fruit Comes From

Use *grow* or *don't grow* to describe which fruits come from Canada.

Tomatoes <u>grow</u> in Canada.

Oranges <u>don't grow</u> in Canada.

Apples <u>grow</u> in Canada.

Look at the picture. Ask and answer questions about fruit in Canada.

A: Do grapefruit grow in Canada?

B: No, they don't grow here.

A: Where do they grow?

B: They grow in _____.

Simple Organisms and Invertebrates

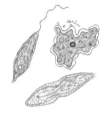

1. protozoa

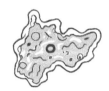

2. amoeba

3. paramecium

4. flatworms

5. roundworms

6. segmented worms

7. earthworm

8. leech

9. jellyfish

10. coral

11. starfish

12. sponge

13. sand dollar

14. sea urchin

Invertebrates

An invertebrate is an animal with no backbone. There are many types of invertebrates. Some are pictured on this page. Other invertebrates include molluscs and insects.

Think about what you know about invertebrates. Create a KWL chart. Fill it in as you learn more.

What I Know	What I Want to Know	What I Learned

Single–Celled Organisms

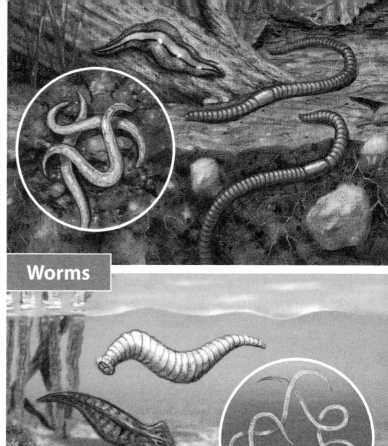

Worms

Ocean Organisms

Molluscs and Crustaceans

 1. octopus

 2. squid

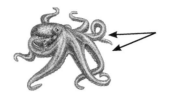 3. tentacles

 4. sea slug

 5. shells

 6. scallop

 7. clam

 8. oyster

 9. mussel

 10. conch

 11. snail

 12. lobster

 13. shrimp

 14. crab

 15. claw

 16. antennae

 17. barnacles

 18. crayfish

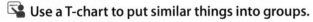

Show Similarities

Use a T-chart to put similar things into groups.

Has Tentacles	Has Antennae
octopus	lobster
squid	crayfish
	shrimp

Look at the T-chart and the pictures. Talk about molluscs and crustaceans.

Examples:

An octopus and a squid have tentacles.

A mussel and a clam have shells.

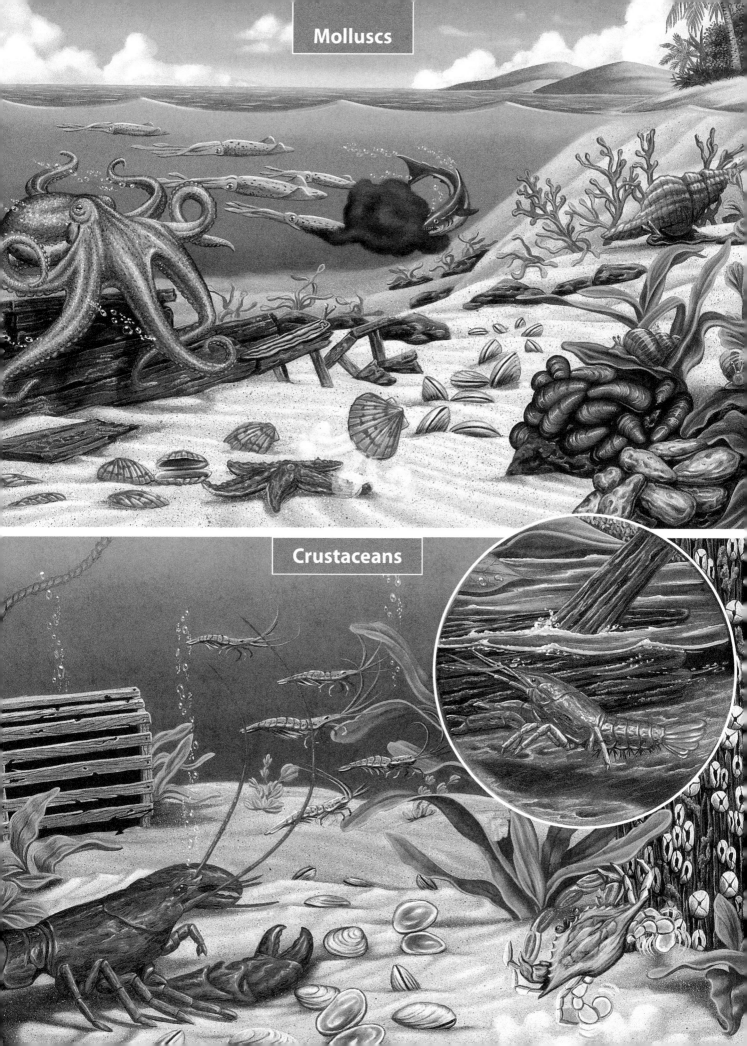

Molluscs

Crustaceans

Insects and Arachnids

 **1.** egg

 **2.** caterpillar

 **3.** chrysalis

 **4.** butterfly

  **5.** metamorphosis

 **6.** hive

 7. bee

 8. ladybug

 **9.** grasshopper

 **10.** cricket

 11. fly

 **12.** firefly

 **13.** mosquito

 14. ant

 15. thorax

 16. abdomen

 **17.** cockroach

 **18.** spider

 **19.** web

 20. tick

 **21.** scorpion

Write about Differences

Use *but* to talk about differences.

Bees live in hives, <u>but</u> spiders do not.

Scorpions have claws, <u>but</u> flies do not.

A ladybug is red, <u>but</u> a bee is yellow.

Ticks are arachnids, <u>but</u> ants are insects.

Look at the pictures. Write about insects and arachnids.

Examples:

A fly has wings, but a spider does not.

A bee is yellow, but a cricket is black.

Insects

Arachnids

Fish

1. bluefish

2. swordfish

3. shark

4. tuna

5. salmon

6. pipefish

7. eel

8. cod

9. sea horse

10. bass

11. minnow

12. trout

13. perch

14. catfish

15. goldfish

16. fin

17. gills

18. scales

Write about How Many

Use *some*, *many*, and *all* to describe how many of something there are.

Some fish are very large.
Many fish are very small.
All fish live in the water.

Look at the pictures. Write about fish.
Examples:
Some fish are freshwater fish.
All fish have gills.

Saltwater Fish

Freshwater Fish

Amphibians and Reptiles

1. salamander

2. frog

3. tadpole

4. toad

5. alligator

6. turtle

7. garter snake

8. chameleon

9. crocodile

10. lizard

11. rattlesnake

12. cobra

13. tail

14. webbed foot

Count Syllables

Words are made up of sound parts. These sound parts are called syllables.

frog	=	frog	=	1 syllable
tadpole	=	tad-pole	=	2 syllables
rattlesnake	=	rat-tle-snake	=	3 syllables
salamander	=	sal-a-man-der	=	4 syllables

Read the amphibian and reptile words out loud. Count the syllables.

Example:

A: tail

B: one syllable

Amphibians

Reptiles

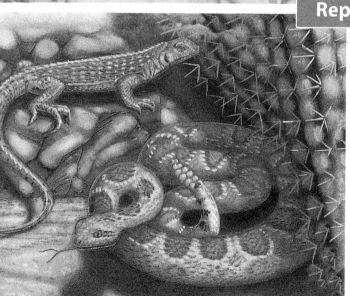

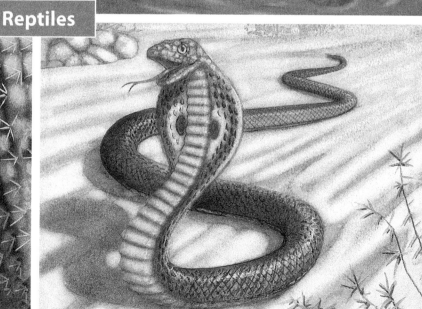

Birds

1. pigeon

2. sparrow

3. robin

4. cardinal

5. goose

6. duck

7. hummingbird

8. crow

9. chicken

10. turkey

11. seagull

12. eagle

13. penguin

14. ostrich

15. peacock

16. parrot

17. beak

18. feather

19. wing

20. nest

Talk about Now

Most birds fly. Use *is flying* to tell where a bird is going now.

The eagle <u>is flying</u> to the nest.

The sparrow <u>is flying</u> into the sky.

The duck <u>is flying</u> from the pond.

Look at the pictures. Talk about birds.
Examples:
The parrot is flying to the branch.
The crow is flying to the farm.

Domestic Mammals

1. dog

2. puppy

3. cat

4. kitten

5. rabbit

6. bunny

7. goat

8. kid

9. sheep

10. lamb

11. cow

12. calf

13. pig

14. piglet

15. horse

16. foal

17. paw

18. forelegs

19. hind legs

20. hoof

Talk about Differences

Add *er* to some adjectives to compare two things.

small + er = smaller

A kid is <u>smaller</u> than a goat.

old + er = older

A sheep is <u>older</u> than a lamb.

Look at the pictures. Talk about domestic animals.

Examples:

A puppy is younger than a dog.

A horse is taller than a foal.

Wild Mammals

1. squirrel

2. bat

3. opossum

4. bear

5. deer

6. skunk

7. raccoon

8. whale

9. dolphin

10. camel

11. kangaroo

12. tiger

13. monkey

14. giraffe

15. lion

16. zebra

17. elephant

18. fur

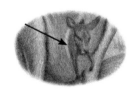

19. pouch

20. tusks

Talk about Needs

Use *has to* or *have to* + a verb to talk about what animals need.

A giraffe <u>has to</u> eat leaves from trees.

A squirrel <u>has to</u> live in a tree.

Zebras <u>have to</u> eat grass.

Whales <u>have to</u> live in the ocean.

Look at the pictures. Talk about wild mammals.

Examples:

Elephants have to have water.

A baby kangaroo has to live in a pouch.

Prehistoric Animals

1. dinosaurs

2. triceratops

3. ankylosaurus

4. apatosaurus

5. anatosaurus

6. diplodocus

7. dryosaurus

8. brachiosaurus

9. stegosaurus

10. tyrannosaurus

11. pteranodon

12. allosaurus

13. smilodon

14. spike

15. sabre tooth

16. fossil

Describe Prehistoric Animals

Use the word *had* to describe prehistoric animals.

The triceratops <u>had</u> three sharp horns.

The diplodocus <u>had</u> a very long tail.

The allosaurus and the smilodon <u>had</u> sharp teeth.

The dryosaurus and the apatosaurus <u>had</u> long necks.

Look at the pictures. Write about prehistoric animals.

Examples:

The stegosaurus had spikes on its tail.

Smilodons had sabre teeth.

Unit 7   Living Things

Herbivores

Carnivores

A Living Things Mind Map

Look at the mind map. Check pages 102–131 to find words you don't know.

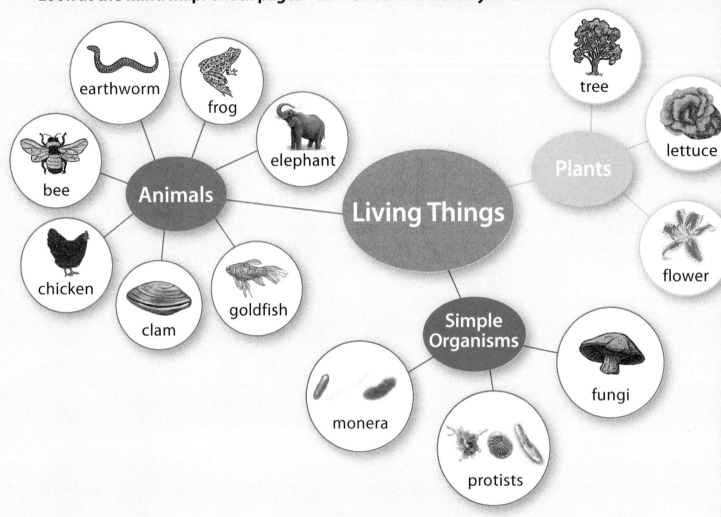

B Use Science Skills

👥 **Read the sentences out loud.**
Point to the pictures in the idea web.

A: A <u>tree</u> is a plant. <u>Lettuce</u> is another plant.

B: A <u>clam</u> is an animal. An <u>earthworm</u> and a <u>bee</u> are animals, too.

A: <u>Monerans</u> and <u>protists</u> are living things.

B: A <u>chicken</u> and a <u>goldfish</u> are animals.

A: A <u>flower</u> is also a plant.

B: A <u>frog</u> is another kind of animal.

C Talk about It

👥 **Ask and answer questions about the idea web. Keep going.**

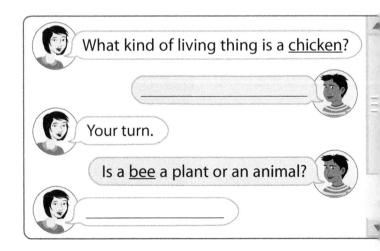

What kind of living thing is a <u>chicken</u>?

_____

Your turn.

Is a <u>bee</u> a plant or an animal?

_____

D Read about It

Living Things

There are many kinds of organisms, or living things. Plants and animals are organisms. Monera, protists, and fungi are also living things.

All organisms are alike in some ways. They need water and food. They grow and change. Organisms make young organisms like themselves.

All organisms are different in some ways, too. Plants and animals are very different. Plants use sunshine to make food. Animals find food to eat. Some animals eat plants. Some animals eat other animals.

Some organisms are not plants or animals. Some of these living things get energy from plants or animals. Some of them get energy from dirt or dead things.

E Check Your Understanding

Read the sentences. Are they *true* or *false*?

1. All organisms need food and water. _T_

2. Organisms do not grow or change. ___

3. Not all living things make young organisms like themselves. ___

4. Animals are not plants. ___

5. Plants eat dirt. ___

6. There are animals that eat other animals. ___

7. Some living things are not plants or animals. ___

8. Some simple organisms get energy from plants. ___

F Write about It

1. Complete a Living Things mind map.

2. Look in your dictionary to find more living things. Write the words or draw pictures in your mind map.

3. Use the information in your mind map. Write about living things.

Example:

Flowers, raccoons, and fungi are living things. A flower is a plant...

G Think about It

👥 **Talk with your class. Answer the questions.**

1. **Inform.** Name three plants that you eat.

2. **Compare and contrast.** How are you like a plant? How are you different from a plant?

3. **Make inferences.** Where can you find living things on Earth? Why do these things live in those places?

Matter and Its Properties

 1. atom

 2. molecule

 3. proton

 4. neutron

 5. electron

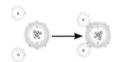 **6. compound**

 **7. element**

 8. mass

 **9. solid**

 **10. liquid**

 **11. gas**

 **12. temperature**

 13. physical change

 **14. chemical change**

 15. solution

 **16. mixture**

 **17. buoyancy**

 **18. freeze**

 **19. melt**

 20. boil

Matter

Matter has three states: solid, liquid, and gas. Sometimes the state of matter changes. For example, when you fill an ice cube tray with water, the water is a liquid. After a few hours, the water freezes and becomes ice. Ice is a solid.

Look around your classroom or your house. Make a list of the liquids and solids you see. Can you see any gases? Do you think there are any gases that you can't see? Add them to the list.

Solid	Liquids	Gases

H₂O

26
Fe
iron

13
Al
aluminum

270g

230°

Sugar

Salt

Flour

Yeast

Forces and Motion

1. inclined plane

2. pulley

3. lever

4. screw

5. wheel and axle

6. wedge

7. acceleration

8. inertia

9. velocity

10. friction

11. gravity

12. speed

13. forces

14. push

15. work

16. pull

Talk about Cause and Effect

Use *when* to show the cause of an effect.

<u>When</u> the car stops, people feel inertia.

<u>When</u> the girl pulls the toy, it rolls.

<u>When</u> the wind blows, the flag waves.

<u>When</u> the worker pushes the cart, it moves.

Look at the pictures. Talk about cause and effect.

Examples:

When the kids skate, the people cheer.

When the man hits the lever, the weights go up.

Speed = 3 m/s

Flight

1. aircraft

2. aerodynamic

3. flight

4. airfoil

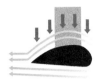
5. pressure

6. drag

7. thrust

8. lift

9. weight/ gravity

10. Bernoulli's Principle

11. propulsion

12. glide

13. pitch

14. roll

15. yaw

16. aileron

17. rudder

18. elevators

19. tail

20. fuselage

21. wings

22. engines

23. propeller

24. flaps

Bernoulli's Principle

Daniel Bernoulli was a Dutch-Swiss mathematician who discovered something important about the way fluids move. He found out that when a fluid (like air) moves faster it applies less pressure to the object it is moving around. This is Bernoulli's Principle.

We use this principle to help make airplanes fly. The wings on a plane are in the shape of an airfoil.

The curve of the airfoil makes air move more quickly over the top of the wing and more slowly underneath it. This means there is more pressure pushing up from below the wing than there is pressure pushing down from the top. This difference produces lift. Lift helps birds and airplanes fly.

Unit 8   The Physical World

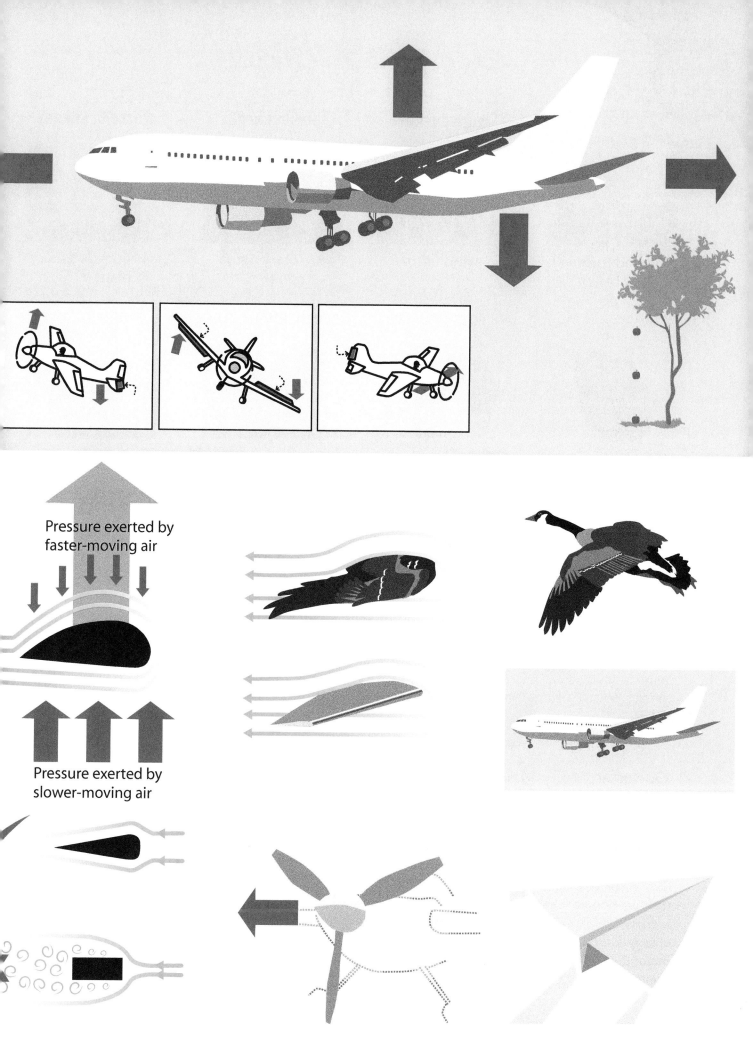

Pressure exerted by
faster-moving air

Pressure exerted by
slower-moving air

Energy and Electricity

WIND ENERGY

1. wind turbine

2. wind farm

SOLAR ENERGY

3. solar energy panel

NUCLEAR ENERGY

4. nuclear power plant

FOSSIL FUELS

5. coal

6. fossil fuels

GEOTHERMAL ENERGY

7. geothermal power plant

HYDROELECTRIC ENERGY

8. hydroelectric power plant

9. potential energy

10. kinetic energy

11. static electricity

12. electrical outlet

13. electric current

14. insulator

15. conductor

16. battery

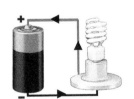

17. electrical circuit

Think about the Topic

Energy can come from many sources. The world's most common sources of energy are fossil fuels. Fossil fuels are popular because large amounts of them exist in parts of the world. Fossil fuels are a non-renewable energy source, however. This means that we will run out of them at some point. We will no longer be able to use fossil fuels.

There are good and bad aspects of all sources of energy. Try to think of some.

Energy Source	Why is using this source of energy good?	Why is using this source of energy bad?
Wind		
Solar		
Nuclear		
Geothermal		
Hydroelectric		

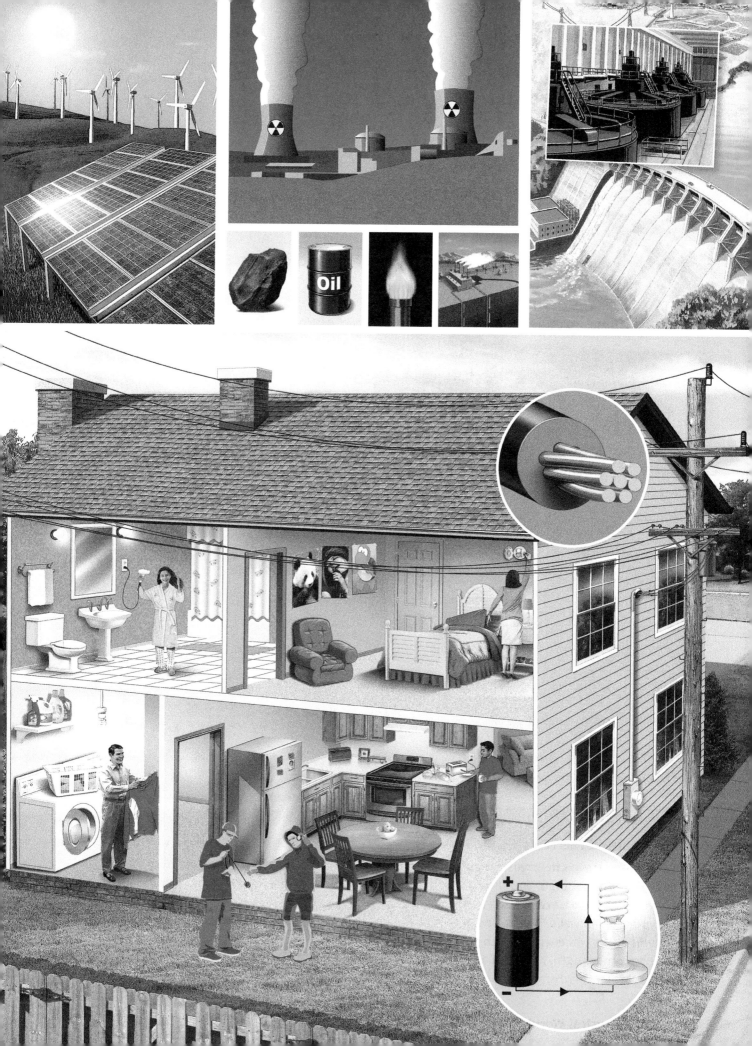

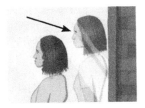

1. radiation

2. conduction

3. convection

4. refraction

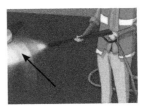

5. reflection

6. vibration

7. visible light

8. translucent

9. transparent

10. opaque

11. longitudinal wave

12. transverse wave

13. crest

14. trough

15. amplitude

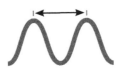

16. wavelength

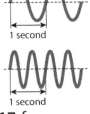

17. frequency

Think about the Topic

Energy travels in waves. Light travels from the sun to your eyes in waves. Light also travels from a lamp to your eyes in waves. Light always travels at the same speed. Each colour of light has its own wavelength, though. For example, violet light has a shorter wavelength than red light.

violet
red

Read the information about light wavelengths again. Think about what you know about the different colours of light. What do you think the wavelengths of green light and yellow light look like? Create a drawing like the one to the left. (Use a prism to help you.)

radio   microwaves   infrared light   visible light   ultraviolet light   X-rays   gamma rays

ON AIR

MENU

A Matter and Energy Mind Map

Look at the mind map. Check pages 134–143 to find words you don't know.

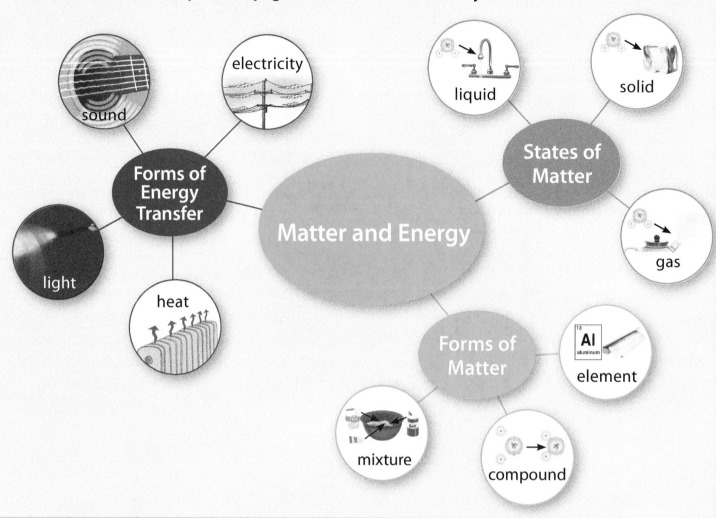

sound

electricity

liquid

solid

Forms of Energy Transfer

States of Matter

Matter and Energy

light

heat

gas

Forms of Matter

13 Al aluminum

element

mixture

compound

B Use Science Skills

👥 **Read the sentences out loud. Point to the pictures in the idea web.**

A: Ice is a <u>solid</u>.

B: <u>Heat</u> is a form of energy transfer.

A: A <u>mixture</u> is a form of matter.

B: <u>Liquid</u> is a state of matter.

A: <u>Electricity</u> is a form of energy transfer.

B: Aluminum is an <u>element</u>.

C Talk about It

👥 **Ask and answer questions about the idea web. Keep going.**

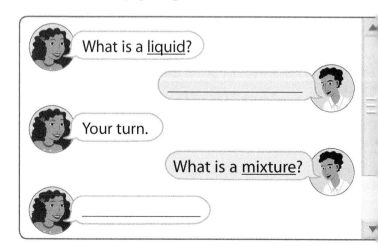

What is a <u>liquid</u>?

_____

Your turn.

What is a <u>mixture</u>?

_____

D Read about It

Matter and Energy

There are different forms of matter. Atoms make up all matter. Matter with only one kind of atom is an element, like iron. Some elements can join together. These joined elements are compounds. Salt and water are compounds. Matter that combines and comes apart forms mixtures. Salt water is a mixture of water and salt.

There are different forms of energy transfer, too. Light, heat, sound, and electricity are types of energy transfer.

Adding or removing energy can change the state of matter. Removing energy from a liquid changes it to a solid. Adding energy to a liquid changes it to a gas.

E Check Your Understanding

Read the sentences. Are they *true* or *false*?

1. Atoms make up matter. __T__

2. Elements have two kinds of atoms. ___

3. Some elements can join together. ___

4. Salt is an element. ___

5. Salt water is not a mixture. ___

6. There are different forms of energy transfer. ___

7. Light is a form of energy transfer. ___

8. Energy cannot change matter. ___

9. Removing energy from a solid makes it a liquid. ___

10. Adding energy to a liquid makes it a gas. ___

F Write about It

1. Complete a Matter and Energy mind map on a piece of paper.

2. Look in your dictionary and other textbooks to find more information about elements, compounds, and mixtures. Add the information to your mind map.

3. Use the information in your mind map. Write about matter and energy.

Example:

Oxygen is an element.
It combines with hydrogen to make water.

G Think about It

👥 **Talk with your class. Answer the questions.**

1. **Classify.** Name something you use at school or at home. Ask your classmates: Is _____ a solid, a liquid, or a gas?

2. **Identify.** What are some ways people use electricity?

3. **Draw conclusions.** Imagine there is a burning candle on a table. After one hour, the candle is only half as tall. Why does the candle get shorter?

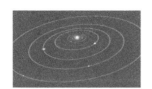
1. galaxy

2. solar system

3. sun

4. planets

5. Mercury

6. Venus

7. Earth

8. Mars

9. Jupiter

10. Saturn

11. Uranus

12. Neptune

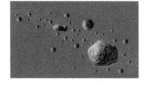
13. moon

14. star

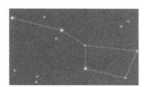
15. constellation

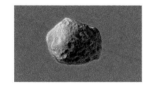
16. comet

17. asteroid belt

18. asteroid

Talk about Part of a Whole

Use *is part of* to talk about one piece of a whole.

A planet <u>is part of</u> a solar system.

A star <u>is part of</u> a constellation.

The sun <u>is part of</u> the universe.

A solar system <u>is part of</u> a galaxy.

Look at the picture. Talk about what you see.
Examples:
Stars are part of a galaxy.
An asteroid is part of an asteroid belt.

The Sun, Earth, and the Moon

1. orbit

2. ellipse

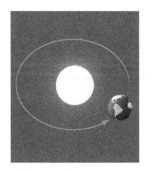

3. revolve

4. axis

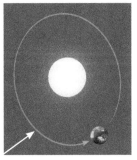

5. tilt

6. rotate

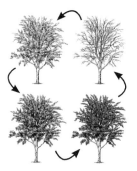

7. seasons

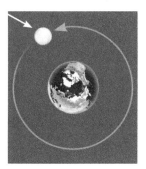

8. satellite

9. tidal bulge

10. high tide

11. low tide

12. moon phases

Think about the Topic

Our seasons are caused by the tilt of the Earth's axis. Summer is warmer than winter because the sun's rays hit the Earth at a more direct angle during summer.

Summer   Earth's orbit   Winter

Sun

Think about Canada's seasons. How might Australia's seasons be different from Canada's? (Use a globe to help you.)

Unit 9   Earth and Space Science

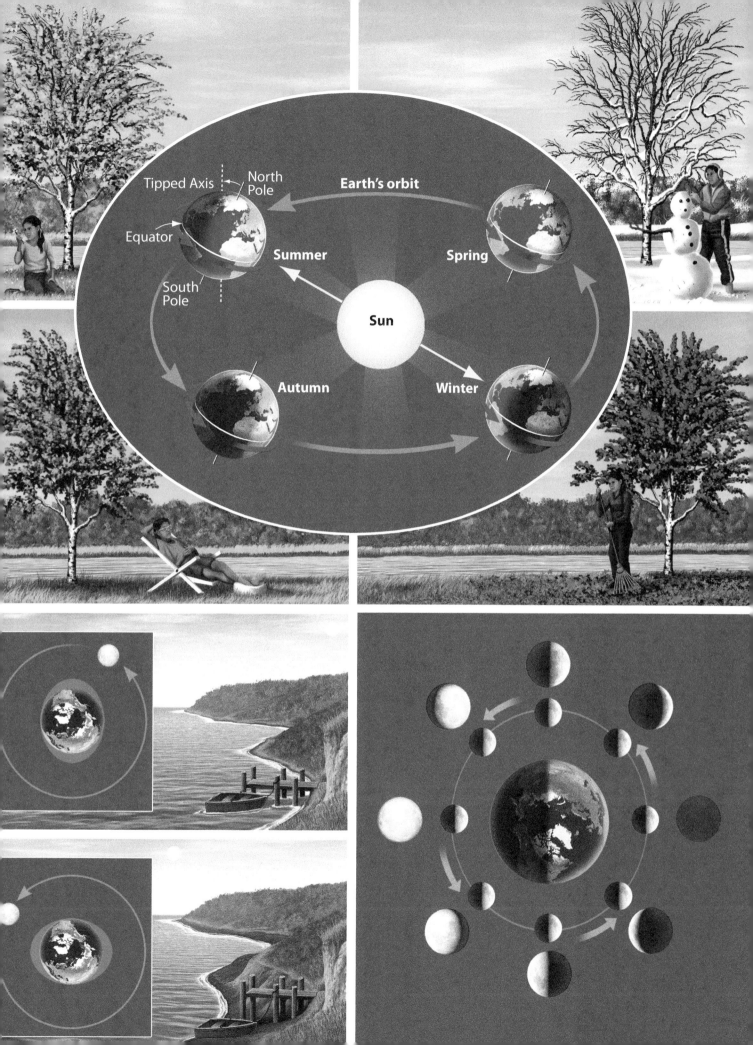

Tipped Axis

North Pole

Equator

South Pole

Earth's orbit

Summer

Spring

Sun

Autumn

Winter

1. mountain

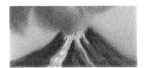
2. volcano

3. lava

4. valley

5. river

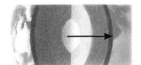
6. glacier

7. plateau

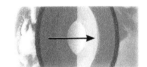
8. ocean

9. layers

10. crust

11. mantle

12. outer core

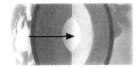
13. inner core

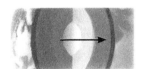
14. erosion

15. weathering

16. sediment

17. sedimentary rock

18. igneous rock

19. metamorphic rock

20. rock cycle

Think about the Topic

Weathering causes rocks to wear down. Many things can cause weathering, including wind and water. When weathering causes bits of rock to break off, these bits are sometimes carried away by the wind or water. This process of carrying the bits away is called erosion.

Can you think of real-life examples of weathering and erosion? Create a chart.

Example of weathering/erosion	What caused this? (wind, water, chemicals, etc.)

Climate Zones and Land Biomes

1. temperate forest

2. taiga

3. tundra

4. tropical rainforest

5. grassland

6. desert

7. deciduous tree

8. evergreen tree

9. moss

10. lichen

11. vines

12. grass

13. sand

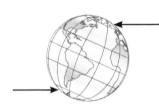
14. polar zones

15. temperate zones

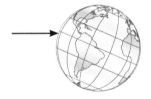
16. tropical zone

Talk about How Often

Use *always*, *usually*, and *never* to explain how often something happens.

Tundra is <u>always</u> very cold.

Grasslands are <u>usually</u> dry.

Tropical rainforests are <u>never</u> cold.

Look at the pictures. Talk about what you see.
Examples:

Deserts are never very rainy.

Evergreen trees are always green.

Unit 9 Earth and Space Science

Temperate forest

Taiga

Tundra

Tropical rainforest

Grassland

Desert

Our Environment
Some Problems and Solutions

 **1.** water pollution

 **2.** air pollution

 **3.** soil pollution

 **4.** runoff pollution

 **5.** smog

 **6.** smoke

 **7.** oil slick

 **8.** exhaust

 **9.** garbage

 **10.** can

 **11.** bottle

 **12.** plastic

 13. glass

 14. metal

 **15.** landfill

 **16.** compost

 **17.** carpool

 **18.** recycle

Talk about Why Things Happen

Use *is caused by* to explain why something happens.

Air pollution <u>is caused by</u> smog.

Soil pollution <u>is caused by</u> garbage.

Exhaust <u>is caused by</u> cars.

Look at the pictures. Talk about what you see.
Examples:

Dead grass is caused by pollution.

Smoke is caused by factories.

Problems

Solutions

Reduce
Reuse
Recycle

Weather

1. atmosphere

2. hurricane

3. rain

4. tornado

5. lightning

6. sunshine

7. cloud

8. wind

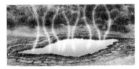

9. evaporation

10. condensation

11. fog

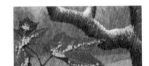

12. water cycle

13. hail

14. weather map

15. blizzard

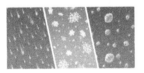

16. sleet

17. snow

18. precipitation

Write about the Weather

Use *was* and *last* to write about weather in the past.

There <u>was</u> a blizzard <u>last</u> Monday.

There <u>was</u> a hurricane <u>last</u> Wednesday.

There <u>was</u> sunshine <u>last</u> Friday.

There <u>was</u> rain <u>last</u> Sunday.

Write about the weather in the past.

Examples:

The weather wasn't nice last week.

There was hail last Thursday.

Unit 9   Earth and Space Science

a evaporation   b condensation

c precipitation   d runoff

St. Paul ☀ 14°

Edmonton ☀ 10°

Wainwright ⛅ 12°

Red Deer 13°

A Our World Cause-and-Effect Chart

Look at the cause-and-effect chart. Check pages 146–157 to find words you don't know.

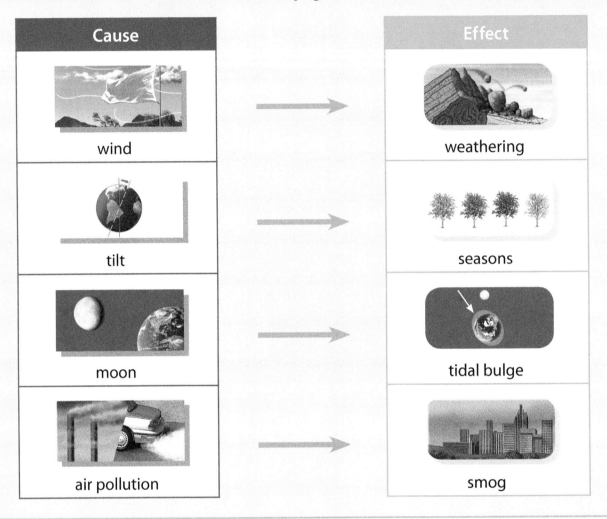

Cause	Effect
wind	weathering
tilt	seasons
moon	tidal bulge
air pollution	smog

B Use Science Skills

👥 **Read the sentences out loud. Point to the pictures in the chart.**

A: The <u>moon</u> causes <u>tidal bulges</u>.

B: <u>Weathering</u> is an effect of <u>wind</u>.

A: Earth's <u>tilt</u> causes <u>seasons</u>.

B: The <u>tidal bulge</u> is an effect of the <u>moon</u>.

A: <u>Air pollution</u> causes <u>smog</u>.

B: <u>Seasons</u> are an effect of Earth's <u>tilt</u>.

C Talk about It

👥 **Ask and answer questions about the chart. Keep going.**

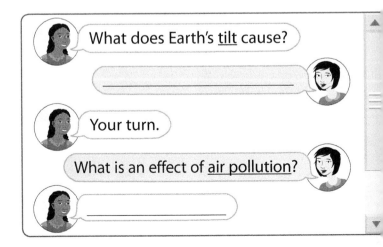

What does Earth's <u>tilt</u> cause?

_____

Your turn.

What is an effect of <u>air pollution</u>?

_____

Our World

There are many causes and effects on Earth. The wind causes weathering. Rocks break into smaller pieces because of wind and other forces.

Some causes and effects are bad. Cars and factories make air pollution. The pollution stays in the air. This causes smog.

Things in space have effects, too. Earth tilts on its axis. The seasons are an effect of this tilt. Seasons change as Earth goes around the sun. The moon causes tidal bulges on Earth. Tidal bulges make the oceans rise and fall.

There are many causes and effects in nature. All of them affect our world.

E Check Your Understanding

Read the sentences. Are they *true* or *false*?

1. There are many causes and effects on Earth. __T__

2. Wind causes weathering. ____

3. Rocks break into pieces because of Earth's tilt. ____

4. Cars and factories cause air pollution. ____

5. Smog is an effect of air pollution. ____

6. Earth's tilt causes oceans to rise and fall. ____

7. Seasons change because of the moon. ____

8. The moon causes tidal bulges. ____

F Write about It

1. Complete a cause-and-effect chart about weather.

2. Look in your dictionary or use the library to find information about causes and effects in the weather. Add them to your chart.

3. Use the information in your chart. Write about some causes and effects in the weather.

Example:

Different kinds of weather have different causes.

Condensation causes fog ...

G Think about It

Talk with your class. Answer the questions.

1. **Make connections**. Name a kind of pollution. Ask your classmates: What is one way to stop _____?

2. **Apply**. Imagine you are outside. There is wind. There are many dark clouds in the sky. What are some weather events that can happen next?

3. **Draw conclusions**. Why do we see the sun rise and set in the sky?

Exploring Math

1. number line

4, 9, 7, 1, 6, 3

2. digits

-4, -3, -2, -1

3. negative numbers

4. even numbers

5. odd numbers

6. add

4 + 1 = 5

7. sum

8. subtract

7 - 3 = 4

9. difference

10. multiply

4 × 3 = 12

11. product

12. divide

6 ÷ 3 = 2

13. quotient

>

14. greater than

<

15. less than

=

16. equals

><=

17. comparisons

1

18. whole number

½

19. fraction

1½

20. mixed numeral

1.5

21. decimal number

Write about Math Symbols

Use these words to describe math symbols.

+	2 + 3	two <u>plus</u> three
−	3 − 2	three <u>minus</u> two
×	2 × 3	two <u>times</u> three
÷	6 ÷ 2	six <u>divided by</u> two
=	2 × 3 = 6	two times three <u>equals</u> six

Write math problems. Then write them with words. Take turns.

Example:

2 + 3 = 5

Two plus three equals five.

Geometry I

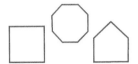 **1.** plane figures

 2. square

 **3.** rectangle

 **4.** triangle

 5. circle

 6. pentagon

 7. octagon

 8. solid figures

 9. cube

 10. sphere

 11. cylinder

 12. cone

 13. rectangular prism

 14. lines

 15. line segment

 16. parallel

 17. perpendicular

 **18.** ray

Describe Shapes

📱 Use *in the shape of* to describe the shape of an object.

The flag is <u>in the shape of</u> a triangle.

The window is <u>in the shape of</u> a square.

A sign is <u>in the shape of</u> a cube.

👥 Look at the picture. Talk about shapes you see.

Examples:

A sign is in the shape of a rectangle.

The wheel is in the shape of a circle.

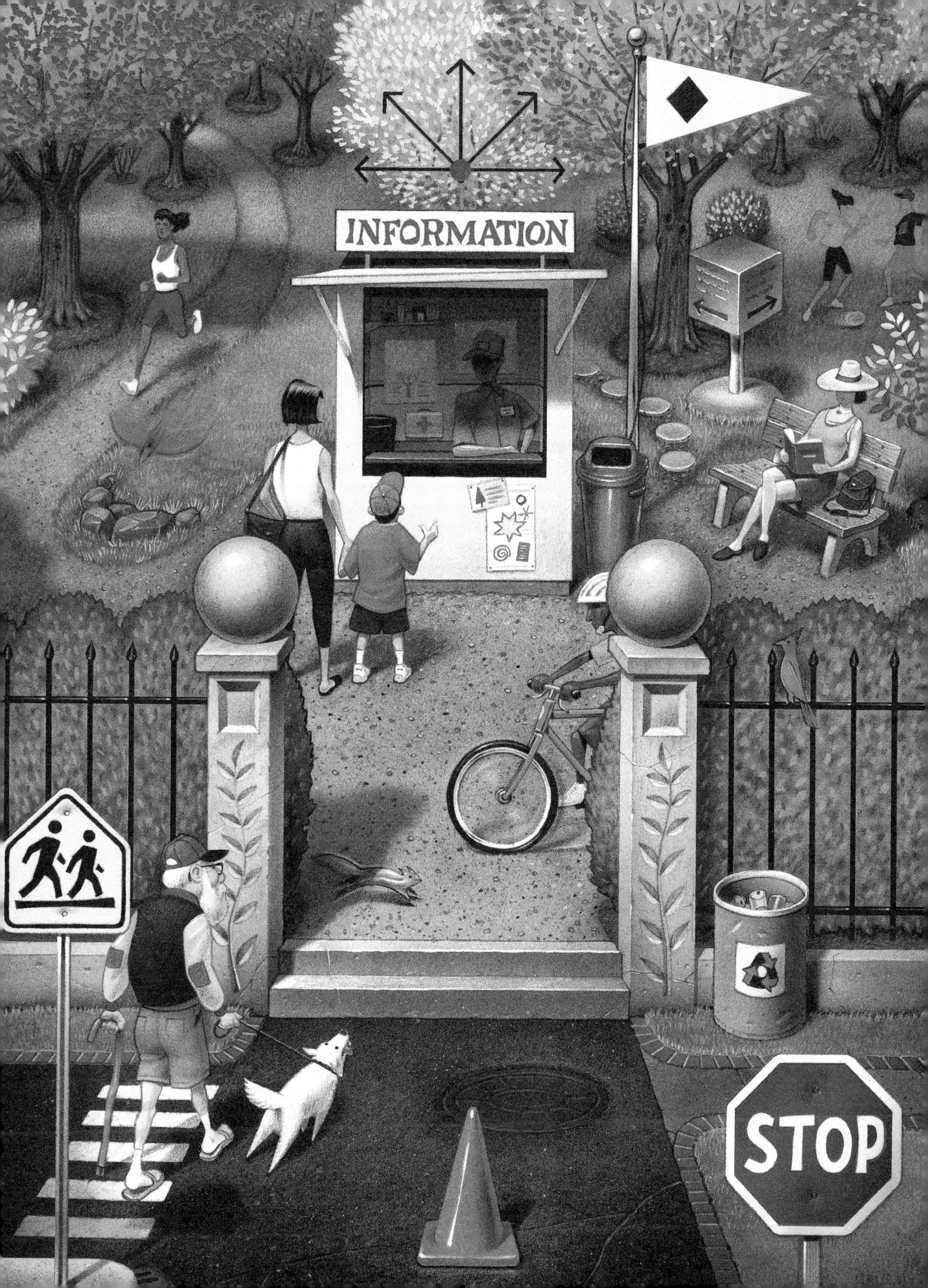
INFORMATION
STOP

Geometry II

 1. symmetrical

 2. asymmetrical

 3. congruent figures

 4. right angle

 5. acute angle

 **6.** obtuse angle

 **7.** straight angle

 8. intersecting lines

 9. circumference

 10. diameter

 11. radius

 12. centre point

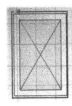 **13.** perimeter

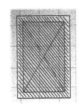 **14.** area

 15. compass

 16. base

 17. edge

 18. face

 19. height

 20. length

 21. width

Show Importance

Use *must* + a verb to talk about something that needs to happen.

She <u>must use</u> a compass to draw a circle.
The model <u>must be</u> three metres wide.
She <u>must measure</u> the height with a ruler.
The plan <u>must show</u> the measurements.

Look at the picture. Talk about what must happen.
Examples:
She must draw the house.
The model must be like the picture.

Measurement

1. millimetre (mm)

2. centimetre (cm)

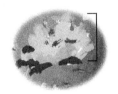
3. decimetre (dm)

4. metre (m)

5. decametre (dam)

6. hectometre (hm)

7. kilometre (km)

8. weight

9. mass

10. milligram (mg)

11. gram (g)

12. kilogram (kg)

13. tonne

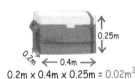
0.25m

0.2m ← 0.4m →
0.2m x 0.4m x 0.25m = 0.02m³
14. volume

1 litre
15. capacity

16. millilitre (mL)

Olive Oil
17. litre (L)

Estimate Measurements

Use *about* to guess measurements.
The beans weigh <u>about</u> half a kilogram.
There is <u>about</u> one tonne of bricks.
The leaf weighs <u>about</u> one gram.
There is <u>about</u> one cup of sugar.

Look at the pictures. Write about measurements you see.
Examples:
There is about one litre of oil.
The garden is about one decametre wide.

Muffins $2.00   Apple Juice $1.00
Cereal $2.50   Orange Juice $1.00
Bread $4.00   Lemonade $1.50

Fresh Herbs and Oils

Number Patterns, Functions, and Relations

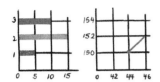

1. graphs

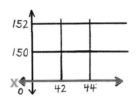

2. *x*-axis

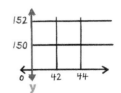

3. *y*-axis

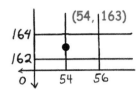

4. coordinates

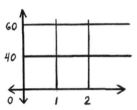

5. coordinate
plane

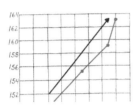

6. ascending
order

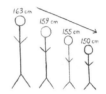

7. descending
order

8. random order

9. Venn diagram

10. table

11. chart

12. sequence

$\{150, 155, 159, 163\}$

13. finite set

$\{150, 152, 154, \ldots\}$

14. infinite set

Basketball	Baseball	Soccer
‖‖‖	‖‖‖	‖‖‖
‖‖‖	‖‖‖	‖‖‖
	‖‖‖	‖‖‖
	‖‖‖	

15. tally chart

Make Words Shorter

Use symbols and abbreviations to make words shorter.

1 centimetre = 1 cm

Ken is <u>150 cm</u> tall.

1 kilogram = 1 kg

Ken weighs <u>44 kg</u>.

Look at the picture. Write about the measurements you see.

Examples:

Anna is 159 cm tall.

Louis weighs 54 kg.

Displaying and Comparing Data

1. population

2. sample

Height of Plants After 30 Days

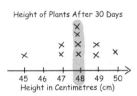

3. mode

42 43 **44** 45 46

4. median

42+43+44+45+46+47+48=315

315 ÷ 7 = 45

5. mean

42+43+44+45+46+47+48=315

48 - 42 = 6

6. range

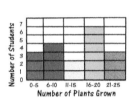

7. bar graph

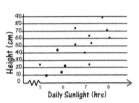

8. scatter plot

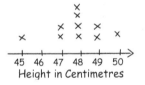

9. line plot

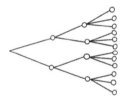

10. pie chart

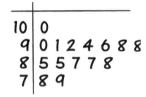

11. tree diagram

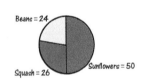

12. stem-and-leaf plot

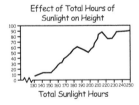

13. line graph

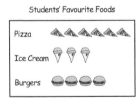

14. pictograph

Use Order Words

🖥 Use *first, next, then,* and *last* to talk about steps in a process.

<u>First,</u> find the population.

<u>Next,</u> take a sample.

<u>Then,</u> put the data in a scatter plot.

<u>Last,</u> find the mean and the median.

👥 Talk about steps to make a bar graph.

First collect information …

Calculators

 **1.** scientific calculator

 **2.** graphing calculator

 SHIFT
3. display

4. second function key

 **5.** square root

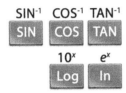 **6.** function keys

 7. negation key

 8. inverse key

 **9.** memory keys

 10. numeric keys

 **11.** operations keys

 **12.** clear key

 13. all clear key

 **14.** exponent key

 15. decimal point key

 **16.** equals key

Give Directions

Use a verb to give directions. This is called an imperative.

<u>Press</u> the clear key.
<u>Enter</u> the numbers.
<u>Use</u> the operations keys.
<u>Find</u> the memory keys.

Give and follow directions to use a calculator.
Examples:
Find the exponent key.
Press a numeric key.

Unit 10 Math and Technology

Computers

1. printer

2. scanner

3. laptop computer

4. touchpad

5. headset

6. microphone

7. PC (personal computer)

8. monitor

9. cursor

10. power switch

11. USB port

12. USB flash drive

13. keyboard

14. mouse

15. cable

16. CD-ROM

17. DVD

18. CD/DVD drive

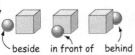

19. webcam

Write about Location

Use *beside, in front of,* and *behind* to describe location.

beside   in front of   behind

The printer is <u>beside</u> the scanner.
The student is <u>in front of</u> the keyboard.
The webcam is <u>behind</u> the DVD.

Look at the picture. Write about what you see.
Examples:
The girl is in front of the printer.
The microphone is beside the laptop.

Unit 10   Math and Technology

Unit 10 Expansion Math and Technology

A Free-time Activities Table and Graph

Look at the table and the graph. Check pages 160–175 to find words you don't know.

Activity	Number of Students
Using the Internet	7
Playing Sports	4
Playing Games	2
Reading Books	5

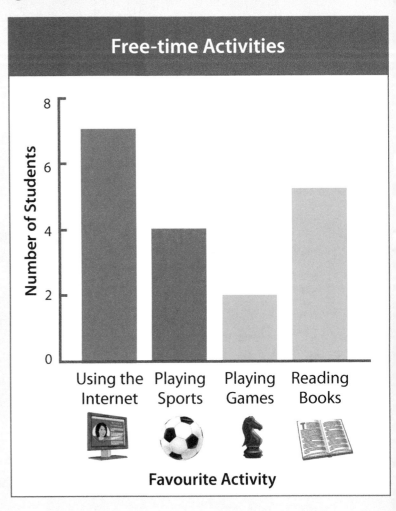

Free-time Activities

B Use Math Skills

👥 **Read the sentences out loud. Point to the information in the table or graph.**

A: The <u>table</u> shows that five students like to read.

B: The <u>bar graph</u> shows that more students like to read than play games.

A: The <u>y-axis</u> has a <u>range</u> of eight.

B: The <u>x-axis</u> shows the favourite activities.

C Talk about It

👥 **Ask and answer questions about the table and the graph. Keep going.**

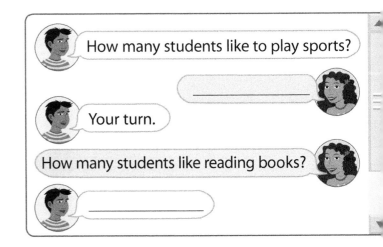

How many students like to play sports?

_____

Your turn.

How many students like reading books?

_____

D Read about It

Free-time Activities

Our class did a project. We asked students about their favourite free-time activities.

We asked a sample of the student population. We charted the answers in a table. The table showed the range of the number of answers. The range was five.

We used the table to make a bar graph. We put the different answers on the x-axis. The numbers of students were on the y-axis. The answers were in random order. The highest number of students with the same answer was seven. Those students like to use the Internet.

We liked this project! We want to do another project like this.

E Check Your Understanding

Read the sentences. Are they *true* or *false*?

1. The project was about free-time activities. _T_

2. They asked the whole student population. ___

3. They did not chart the answers. ___

4. The table showed the range. ___

5. The range was seven. ___

6. They used the table information to make a bar graph. ___

7. The different answers were on the x-axis. ___

8. Seven students like to use the Internet. ___

F Write about It

1. Make a Free-time Activities table. Ask five students in your class to name their favourite free-time activities. Write the students' answers in the table.

2. Use the information in your table to make a graph. Make a bar graph or another kind of graph.

3. Write about how you made your Free-time Activities graph.

Example:

I asked five students about their favourite free-time activities.

They named four activities ...

G Think about It

👥 **Talk with your class. Answer the questions.**

1. **Make connections.** Computers and calculators are important tools. How can you use a computer or calculator to help you display data?

2. **Explain.** Which kind of graph is the easiest to read and understand? Why?

3. **Apply.** You want to show how PCs and laptops are different and how they are similar. What kind of graph or diagram do you use? Why?

Time

Day

morning   noon   afternoon

Night

evening   midnight

Money

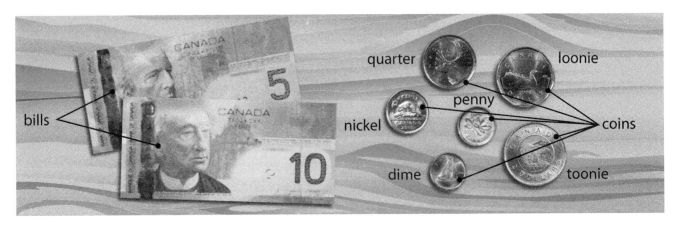

bills

quarter   loonie

nickel   penny

dime   toonie

coins

The Calendar

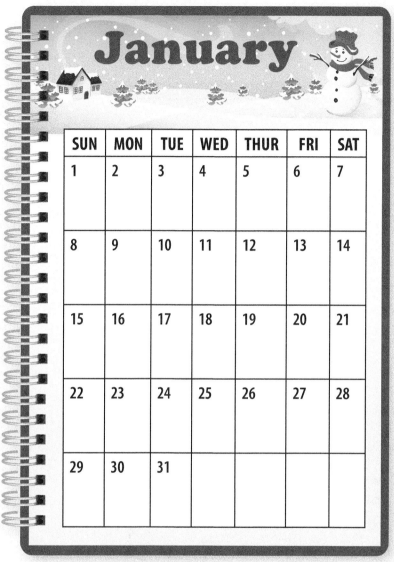

Months

January	February
March	April
May	June
July	August
September	October
November	December

The Days of the Week

Sunday Monday Tuesday Wednesday Thursday Friday Saturday

Ordinal numbers

first second third fourth fifth sixth seventh eighth ninth tenth

Opposites

right

left

large

small

tall

short

thin

thick

high

low

full

empty

closed

open

old

new

clean

dirty

Clothing

raincoat

ski cap

scarf

jacket

mittens

gloves

dress

ring

baseball cap

sweatshirt

jeans

boots

running shoes

T-shirt

sweater

sweatpants

earrings

shirt

tie

coat

bathrobe

pyjamas

blouse

skirt

belt

suit

shorts

bracelet

underwear

tights

pants

slippers

nightgown

underpants

shoes

socks

World Map

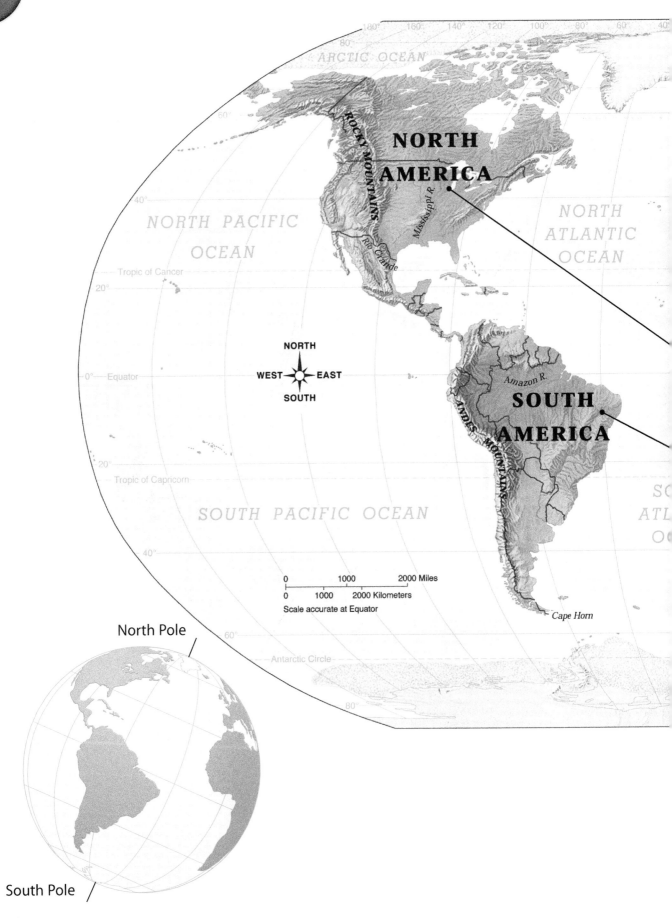

ARCTIC OCEAN

ROCKY MOUNTAINS

NORTH AMERICA

NORTH PACIFIC OCEAN

Mississippi R.

Rio Grande

NORTH ATLANTIC OCEAN

Tropic of Cancer

NORTH
WEST — EAST
SOUTH

Equator

Amazon R.

SOUTH AMERICA

ANDES MOUNTAINS

SO
ATL
OC

Tropic of Capricorn

SOUTH PACIFIC OCEAN

0   1000   2000 Miles
0   1000   2000 Kilometers
Scale accurate at Equator

Cape Horn

North Pole

Antarctic Circle

South Pole

182 Appendix

ARCTIC OCEAN

Circle

URAL MTS.

Volga R.

Ob R.

EUROPE

ALPS

ASIA

MTS.

Nile R.

HIMALAYAS

Indus R.

Ganges R.

Yangtze R.

Niger R.

PACIFIC OCEAN

AFRICA

INDIAN OCEAN

AUSTRALIA

Cape of
Good Hope

ANTARCTICA

continents

Index

The number(s) to the right of each entry show the page(s) on which the term is found. Terms with page numbers in blue appear in a topic's title or can be found as labels or text within an illustration.